Christopher Columbus
And The New World Of His Discovery
Volume 7

FILSON YOUNG

[ZHINGOORA BOOKS]

This edition is published by
Zhingoora Books.

Apart from any fair dealing for the purposes of research or private study, or criti-cism or review, this publication may only be reproduced, stored or transmitted, in any form or by any means, with the prior permission in writing of the publishers. All disputes are subject to exclusive jurisdiction of Mandsaur Courts only. For any suggestions and feedback or book on new concept/domain, please contact us at the email given below.

contact@Zhingoora.com

About Author

Alexander Bell Filson Young was a journalist, BBC programme advisor and author. His wrote the book on Titanic, a RMS Titanic ship. His famous works includeTitanic, The Relief of Mafekingand etc.

CHAPTER I

DEGRADATION

The first things seen by Francisco de Bobadilla when he entered the harbour of San Domingo on the morning of the 23rd of August 1500 were the bodies of several Spaniards, hanging from a gibbet near the water-side —a grim confirmation of what he had heard about the troubled state of the island. While he was waiting for the tide so that he might enter the harbour a boat put off from shore to ascertain who was on board the caravels; and it was thus informally that Bobadilla first announced that he had come to examine into the state of the island. Columbus was not at San Domingo, but was occupied in settling the affairs of the Vega Real; Bartholomew also was absent, stamping out the last smouldering embers of rebellion in Xaragua; and only James was in command to deal with this awkward situation.

Bobadilla did not go ashore the first day, but remained on board his ship receiving the visits of various discontented colonists who, getting early wind of the purpose of his visit, lost no time in currying favour with him, Probably he heard enough that first day to have damned the administration of a dozen islands; but also we must allow him some interest in the wonderful and strange sights that he was seeing; for Espanola, which has perhaps grown wearisome to us, was new to him. He had brought with him an armed body-guard of twenty-five men, and in the other caravel were the returned slaves, babies and all, under the charge of six friars. On the day following his arrival Bobadilla landed and heard mass in state, afterwards reading out his commission to the assembled people. Evidently he had received a shocking impression of the state of affairs in the island; that is the only explanation of the action suddenly taken by him, for his first public act was to demand from James the release of all the prisoners in the fortress, in order that they and their accusers should appear before him.

James is in a difficulty; and, mule-like, since he does not know which way to turn, stands stock still. He can do nothing, he says, without the Admiral's consent. The next day Bobadilla, again hearing mass in state, causes further documents to be read showing that a still greater degree of power had been entrusted to his hands. Mule-like, James still stands stock still; the greatest power on earth known to him is his eldest brother, and he will not, positively dare not, be moved by anything less than that. He refuses to give up the prisoners on any grounds whatsoever, and Bobadilla has to take the fortress by assault—an easy enough matter since the resistance is but formal.

The next act of Bobadilla's is not quite so easy to understand. He quartered himself in Columbus's house; that perhaps was reasonable enough since there may not have been another house in the settlement fit to receive him; but he also, we are told, took possession of all his papers, public and private, and also seized the Admiral's store of money and began to pay his debts with it for him, greatly to the satisfaction of San Domingo. There is an element of the comic in this interpretation of a commissioner's powers; and it seemed as though he meant to wind up the whole Columbus business, lock, stock, and barrel. It would not be in accordance with our modern ideas of honour that a man's private papers should be seized unless he were suspected of treachery or some criminal act; but apparently Bobadilla regarded it as necessary. We must remember that although he had only heard one side of the case it was evidently so positive, and the fruits of misgovernment were there so visibly before his eyes, that no amount of evidence in favour of Columbus would make him change his mind as to his fitness to govern. Poor James, witnessing these things and unable to do anything to prevent them, finds himself suddenly relieved from the tension of the situation. Since inaction is his note, he shall be indulged in it; and he is clapped in irons and cast into prison. James can hardly believe the evidence of his senses. He has been studying theology lately, it appears, with a view to entering the Church and perhaps being some day made Bishop of Espanola, but this new turn of affairs looks as though there were to be an end of all careers for him, military and ecclesiastical alike.

Christopher at Fort Concepcion had early news of the arrival of Bobadilla, but in the hazy state of his mind he did not regard it as an event of sufficient importance to make his immediate presence at San Domingo advisable. The name of Bobadilla conveyed nothing to him; and when he heard that he had come to investigate, he thought that he came to set right some disputed questions between the Admiral and other navigators as to the right of visiting Espanola and the Paria coast. As the days went on, however, he heard more disquieting rumours; grew at last uneasy, and moved to a fort nearer San Domingo in case it should be necessary for him to go there. An officer met him on the road bearing the proclamations issued by Bobadilla, but not the message from the Sovereigns requiring the Admiral's obedience to the commissioner. Columbus wrote to the commissioner a curious letter, which is not preserved, in which he sought to gain time; excusing himself from responsibility for the condition of the island, and assuring Bobadilla that, as he intended to return to Spain almost immediately, he (Bobadilla) would have ample opportunity for exercising his command in his absence. He also wrote to the Franciscan friars who had accompanied Bobadilla asking them to use their influence—the Admiral having some vague connection with the Franciscan order since his days at La Rabida.

No reply came to any of these letters, and Columbus sent word that he still regarded his authority as paramount in the island. For reply to this he received the Sovereigns' message to him which we have seen, commanding him to put himself under the direction of Bobadilla. There was no mistaking this; there was the order in plain words; and with I know not what sinkings of heart Columbus at last set out for San Domingo. Bobadilla had expected resistance, but the Admiral, whatever his faults, knew how to behave with, dignity in a humiliating position; and he came into the city unattended on August 23, 1500. On the outskirts of the town he was met by Bobadilla's guards, arrested, put in chains, and lodged in the fortress, the tower of which exists to this day. He seemed to himself to be the victim of a particularly petty and galling kind of treachery, for it was his own cook, a man called Espinoza, who riveted his gyves upon him.

There remained Bartholomew to be dealt with, and he, being at large and in command of the army, might not have proved such an easy conquest, but that Christopher, at Bobadilla's request, wrote and advised him to submit to arrest without any resistance. Whether Bartholomew acquiesced or not is uncertain; what is certain is that he also was captured and placed in irons, and imprisoned on one of the caravels. James in one caravel, Bartholomew in another, and Christopher in the fortress, and all in chains—this is what it has come to with the three sons of old Domenico.

The trial was now begun, if trial that can be called which takes place in the absence of the culprit or his representative. It was rather the hearing of charges against Christopher and his brothers; and we may be sure that every discontented feeling in the island found voice and was formulated into some incriminating charge. Columbus was accused of oppressing the Spanish settlers by making them work at harsh and unnecessary labour; of cutting down their allowance of food, and restricting their liberty; of punishing them cruelly and unduly; of waging wars unjustly with the natives; of interfering with the conversion of the natives by hastily collecting them and sending them home as slaves; of having secreted treasures which should have been delivered to the Sovereigns—this last charge, like some of the others, true. He had an accumulation of pearls of which he had given no account to Fonseca, and the possession of which he excused by the queer statement that he was waiting to announce it until he could match it with an equal amount of gold! He was accused of hating the Spaniards, who were represented as having risen in the late rebellion in order to protect the natives and avenge their own wrongs—, and generally of having abused his office in order to enrich his own family and gratify his own feelings. Bobadilla appeared to believe all these charges; or perhaps he recognised their nature, and yet saw that there was a sufficient degree of truth in them to disqualify the Admiral in his position as Viceroy. In all these affairs his right-hand man was Roldan, whose loyalty to Columbus, as we foresaw, had been short-lived. Roldan collects evidence; Roldan knows where he can lay his hands on this witness; Roldan produces this and that proof; Roldan is here, there, and everywhere—never had Bobadilla found such a useful, obliging man as Roldan. With his help Bobadilla soon collected a sufficient weight of evidence to justify in his own mind his sending Columbus home to Spain, and remaining himself in command of the island.

The caravels having been made ready, and all the evidence drawn up and documented, it only remained to embark the prisoners and despatch them to Spain. Columbus, sitting in his dungeon, suffering from gout and ophthalmic as well as from misery and humiliation, had heard no news; but he had heard the shouting of the people in the streets, the beating of drums and blowing of horns, and his own name and that of his brothers uttered in derision; and he made sure that he was going to be executed. Alonso de Villegio, a nephew of Bishop Fonseca's, had been appointed to take charge of the ships returning to Spain; and when he came into the prison the Admiral thought his last hour had come.

"Villegio," he asked sadly, "where are you taking me?"

"I am taking you to the ship, your Excellency, to embark," replied the other.

"To embark?" repeated the Admiral incredulously. "Villegio! are you speaking the truth?"

"By the life of your Excellency what I say is true," was the reply, and the news came with a wave of relief to the panic-stricken heart of the Admiral.

In the middle of October the caravels sailed from San Domingo, and the last sounds heard by Columbus from the land of his discovery were the hoots and jeers and curses hurled after him by the treacherous, triumphant rabble on the shore. Villegio treated him and his brothers with as much kindness as possible, and offered, when they had got well clear of Espanola, to take off the Admiral's chains. But Columbus, with a fine counterstroke of picturesque dignity, refused to have them removed. Already, perhaps, he had realised that his subjection to this cruel and quite unnecessary indignity would be one of the strongest things in his favour when he got to Spain, and he decided to suffer as much of it as he could. "My Sovereigns commanded me to submit to what Bobadilla should order. By his authority I wear these chains, and I shall continue to wear them until they are removed by order of the

Sovereigns; and I will keep them afterwards as reminders of the reward I have received for my services." Thus the Admiral, beginning to pick up his spirits again, and to feel the better for the sea air.

The voyage home was a favourable one and in the course of it Columbus wrote the following letter to a friend of his at Court, Dona Juana de la Torre, who had been nurse to Prince Juan and was known by him to be a favourite of the Queen:

"MOST VIRTUOUS LADY,—Though my complaint of the world is new, its habit of ill-using is very ancient. I have had a thousand struggles with it, and have thus far withstood them all, but now neither arms nor counsels avail me, and it cruelly keeps me under water. Hope in the Creator of all men sustains me: His help was always very ready; on another occasion, and not long ago, when I was still more overwhelmed, He raised me with His right arm, saying, 'O man of little faith, arise: it is I; be not afraid.'

"I came with so much cordial affection to serve these Princes, and have served them with such service, as has never been heard of or seen.

"Of the new heaven and earth which our Lord made, when Saint John was writing the Apocalypse, after what was spoken by the mouth of Isaiah, He made me the messenger, and showed me where it lay. In all men there was disbelief, but to the Queen, my Lady, He gave the spirit of understanding, and great courage, and made her heiress of all, as a dear and much loved daughter. I went to take possession of all this in her royal name. They sought to make amends to her for the ignorance they had all shown by passing over their little knowledge and talking of obstacles and expenses. Her Highness, on the other hand, approved of it, and supported it as far as she was able.

"Seven years passed in discussion and nine in execution. During this time very remarkable and noteworthy things occurred whereof no idea at all had been formed. I have arrived at, and am in, such a condition that there is no person so vile but thinks he may insult me: he shall be reckoned in the world as valour itself who is courageous enough not to consent to it.

"If I were to steal the Indies or the land which lies towards them, of which I am now speaking, from the altar of Saint Peter, and give them to the Moors, they could not show greater enmity towards me in Spain. Who would believe such a thing where there was always so much magnanimity?

"I should have much desired to free myself from this affair had it been honourable towards my Queen to do so. The support of our Lord and of her Highness made me persevere: and to alleviate in some measure the sorrows which death had caused her, I undertook a fresh voyage to the new heaven and earth which up to that time had remained hidden; and if it is not held there in esteem like the other voyages to the Indies, that is no wonder, because it came to be looked upon as my work.

"The Holy Spirit inflamed Saint Peter and twelve others with him, and they all contended here below, and their toils and hardships were many, but last of all they gained the victory.

"This voyage to Paria I thought would somewhat appease them on account of the pearls, and of the discovery of gold in Espanola. I ordered the pearls to be collected and fished for by people with whom an arrangement was made that I should return for them, and, as I understood, they were to be measured by the bushel. If I did not write about this to their Highnesses, it was because I wished to have first of all done the same thing with the gold.

"The result to me in this has been the same as in many other things; I should not have lost them nor my honour, if I had sought my own advantage, and had allowed Espanola to be ruined, or if my privileges and contracts had been observed. And I say just the same about the gold which I had then collected, and [for] which with such great afflictions and toils I have, by divine power, almost perfected [the arrangements].

"When I went from Paria I found almost half the people from Espanola in revolt, and they have waged war against me until now, as against a Moor; and the Indians on the other side grievously [harassed me]. At this time Hojeda arrived and tried to put the finishing stroke: he said that their Highnesses had sent him with promises of gifts, franchises and pay: he gathered together a great band, for in the whole of Espanola there are very few save vagabonds, and not one with wife and children. This Hojeda gave me great trouble; he was obliged to depart, and left word that he would soon return with more ships and people, and that he had left the Royal person of the Queen, our Lady, at the point of death. Then Vincente Yanez arrived with four caravels; there was disturbance and mistrust but no mischief: the Indians talked of many others at the Cannibals [Caribbee Islands] and in Paria; and afterwards spread the news of six other caravels, which were brought by a brother of the Alcalde, but it was with malicious intent. This occurred at the very last, when the hope that their

Highnesses would ever send any ships to the Indies was almost abandoned, nor did we expect them; and it was commonly reported that her Highness was dead.

"A certain Adrian about this time endeavoured to rise in rebellion again, as he had done previously, but our Lord did not permit his evil purpose to succeed. I had purposed in myself never to touch a hair of anybody's head, but I lament to say that with this man, owing to his ingratitude, it was not possible to keep that resolve as I had intended: I should not have done less to my brother, if he had sought to kill me, and steal the dominion which my King and Queen had given me in trust.

"This Adrian, as it appears, had sent Don Ferdinand to Xaragua to collect some of his followers, and there a dispute arose with the Alcalde from which a deadly contest ensued, and he [Adrian] did not effect his purpose. The Alcalde seized him and a part of his band, and the fact was that he would have executed them if I had not prevented it; they were kept prisoners awaiting a caravel in which they might depart. The news of Hojeda which I told them made them lose the hope that he would now come again.

"For six months I had been prepared to return to their Highnesses with the good news of the gold, and to escape from governing a dissolute people Who fear neither God nor their King and Queen, being full of vices and wickedness.

"I could have paid the people in full with six hundred thousand, and for this purpose I had four millions of tenths and somewhat more, besides the third of the gold.

"Before my departure I many times begged their Highnesses to send there, at my expense, some one to take charge of the administration of justice; and after finding the Alcalde in arms I renewed my supplications to have either some troops or at least some servant of theirs with letters patent; for my reputation is such that even if I build churches and hospitals, they will always be called dens of thieves.

"They did indeed make provision at last, but it was the very contrary of what the matter demanded: it may be successful, since it was according to their good pleasure.

"I was there for two years without being able to gain a decree of favour for myself or for those who went there, yet this man brought a coffer full: whether they will all redound to their [Highnesses] service, God knows. Indeed, to begin with, there are exemptions for twenty years, which is a man's lifetime; and gold is collected to such an extent that there was one person who became worth five marks in four hours; whereof I will speak more fully later on.

"If it would please their Highnesses to remove the grounds of a common saying of those who know my labours, that the calumny of the people has done me more harm than much service and the maintenance of their [Highnesses] property and dominion has done me good, it would be a charity, and I should be re-established in my honour, and it would be talked about all over the world: for the undertaking is of such a nature that it must daily become more famous and in higher esteem.

"When the Commander Bobadilla came to Santo Domingo, I was at La Vega, and the Adelantado at Xaragua, where that Adrian had made a stand, but then all was quiet, and the land rich and all men at peace. On the second day after his arrival, he created himself Governor, and appointed officers and made executions, and proclaimed immunities of gold and tenths and in general of everything else for twenty years, which is a man's lifetime, and that he came to pay everybody in full up to that day, even though they had not rendered service; and he publicly gave notice that, as for me, he had charge to send me in irons, and my brothers likewise, as he has done, and that I should nevermore return thither, nor any other of my family: alleging a thousand disgraceful and discourteous things about me. All this took place on the second day after his arrival, as I have said, and while I was absent at a distance, without my knowing either of him or of his arrival.

"Some letters of their Highnesses signed in blank, of which he brought a number, he filled up and sent to the Alcalde and to his company with favours and commendations: to me he never sent either letter or messenger, nor has he done so to this day. Imagine what any one holding my office would think when one who endeavoured to rob their Highnesses, and who has done so much evil and mischief, is honoured and favoured, while he who maintained it at such risks is degraded.

"When I heard this I thought that this affair would be like that of Hojeda or one of the others, but I restrained myself when I learnt for certain from the friars that their Highnesses had sent him. I wrote to him that his arrival was welcome, and that I was prepared to go to the Court and had sold all I possessed by auction; and that with respect to the immunities he should not be hasty, for both that matter and the government I would hand over to him immediately as smooth as my palm. And I wrote to the same effect to the friars, but neither he nor they gave me any answer. On the contrary, he put himself in a warlike attitude, and compelled all who went there to take an oath to him as Governor; and they told me that it was for twenty years.

"Directly I knew of those immunities, I thought that I would repair such a great error and that he would be pleased, for he gave them without the need or occasion necessary in so vast a matter: and he gave to vagabond people what would have been excessive for a man who had brought wife and children. So I announced by word and letters that he could not use his patents because mine were those in force; and I showed them the immunities which John Aguado brought.

"All this was done by me in order to gain time, so that their Highnesses might be informed of the condition of the country, and that they might have an opportunity of issuing fresh commands as to what would best promote their service in that respect.

"It is useless to publish such immunities in the Indies: to the settlers who have taken up residence it is a pure gain, for the best lands are given to them, and at a low valuation they will be worth two-hundred thousand at the end of the four years when the period of residence is ended, without their digging a spadeful in them. I would not speak thus if the settlers were married, but there are not six among them all who are not on the look-out to gather what they can and depart speedily. It would be a good thing if they should go from Castile, and also if it were known who and what they are, and if the country could be settled with honest people.

"I had agreed with those settlers that they should pay the third of the gold, and the tenths, and this at their own request; and they received it as a great favour from their Highnesses. I reproved them when I heard that they ceased to do this, and hoped that the Commander would do likewise, and he did the contrary.

"He incensed them against me by saying that I wanted to deprive them of what their Highnesses had given them; and he endeavoured to set them at variance with me, and did so; and he induced them to write to their Highnesses that they should never again send me back to the government, and I likewise make the same supplication to them for myself and for my whole family, as long as there are not different inhabitants. And he together with them ordered inquisitions concerning me for wickednesses the like whereof were never known in hell. Our Lord, who rescued Daniel and the three children, is present with the same wisdom and power as He had then, and with the same means, if it should please Him and be in accordance with His will.

"I should know how to remedy all this, and the rest of what has been said and has taken place since I have been in the Indies, if my disposition would allow me to seek my own advantage, and if it seemed honourable to me to do so, but the maintenance of justice and the extension of the dominion of her Highness has hitherto kept me down. Now that so much gold is found, a dispute arises as to which brings more profit, whether to go about robbing or to go to the mines. A hundred castellanos are as easily obtained for a woman as for a farm, and it is very general, and there are plenty of dealers who go about looking for girls: those from nine to ten are now in demand, and for all ages a good price must be paid.

"I assert that the violence of the calumny of turbulent persons has injured me more than my services have profited me; which is a bad example for the present and for the future. I take my oath that a number of men have gone to the Indies who did not deserve water in the sight of God and of the world; and now they are returning thither, and leave is granted them.

"I assert that when I declared that the Commander could not grant immunities, I did what he desired, although I told him that it was to cause delay until their Highnesses should, receive information from the country, and should command anew what might be for their service.

"He excited their enmity against me, and he seems, from what took place and from his behaviour, to have come as my enemy and as a very vehement one; or else the report is true that he has spent much to obtain this employment. I do not know more about it than what I hear. I never heard of an inquisitor gathering rebels together and accepting them, and others devoid of credit and unworthy of it, as witnesses against their Governor.

"If their Highnesses were to make a general inquisition there, I assure you that they would look upon it as a great wonder that the island does not founder.

"I think your Ladyship will remember that when, after losing my sails, I was driven into Lisbon by a tempest, I was falsely accused of having gone there to the King in order to give him the Indies. Their Highnesses afterwards learned the contrary, and that it was entirely malicious.

"Although I may know but little, I do not think any one considers me so stupid as not to know that even if the Indies were mine I could not uphold myself without the help of some Prince.

"If this be so, where could I find better support and security than in the King and Queen, our Lords, who have raised me from nothing to such great honour, and are the most exalted Princes of the world on sea and on land, and who consider that I have rendered them service, and who preserve to me my privileges and rewards: and if any one infringes them, their Highnesses increase them still more, as was seen in the case of John Aguado; and they order great honour to be conferred upon me, and, as I have already said, their Highnesses have received service from me, and keep my sons in their household; all which could by no means happen with another prince, for where there is no affection, everything else fails.

"I have now spoken thus in reply to a malicious slander, but against my will, as it is a thing which should not recur to memory even in dreams; for the Commander Bobadilla maliciously seeks in this way to set his own conduct and actions in a brighter light; but I shall easily show him that his small knowledge and great cowardice, together with his inordinate cupidity, have caused him to fail therein.

"I have already said that I wrote to him and to the friars, and immediately set out, as I told him, almost alone, because all the people were with the Adelantado, and likewise in order to prevent suspicion on his part. When he heard this, he seized Don Diego and sent him on board a caravel loaded with irons, and did the same to me upon my arrival, and afterwards to the Adelantado when he came; nor did I speak to him any more, nor to this day has he allowed any one to speak to me; and I take my oath that I cannot understand why I am made a prisoner.

"He made it his first business to seize the gold, which he did without measuring or weighing it and in my absence; he said that he wanted it to pay the people, and according to what I hear he assigned the chief part to himself and sent fresh exchangers for the exchanges. Of this gold I had put aside certain specimens, very big lumps, like the eggs of geese, hens, and pullets, and of many other shapes, which some persons had collected in a short space of time, in order that their Highnesses might be gladdened, and might comprehend the business upon seeing a quantity of large stones full of gold. This collection was the first to be given away, with malicious intent, so that their Highnesses should not hold the matter in any account until he has feathered his nest, which he is in great haste to do. Gold which is for melting diminishes at the fire: some chains which would weigh about twenty marks have never been seen again.

"I have been more distressed about this matter of the gold than even about the pearls, because I have not brought it to her Highness.

"The Commander at once set to work upon anything which he thought would injure me. I have already said that with six hundred thousand I could pay every one without defrauding anybody, and that I had more than four millions of tenths and constabulary [dues] without touching the gold. He made some free gifts which are ridiculous, though I believe that he began by assigning the chief part to himself. Their

Highnesses will find it out when they order an account to be obtained from him, especially if I should be present thereat. He does nothing but reiterate that a large sum is owing, and it is what I have said, and even less. I have been much distressed that there should be sent concerning me an inquisitor who is aware that if the inquisition which he returns is very grave he will remain in possession of the government.

"Would that it had pleased our Lord that their Highnesses had sent him or some one else two years ago, for I know that I should now be free from scandal and infamy, and that my honour would not be taken from me, nor should I lose it. God is just, and will make known the why and the wherefore.

"They judge me over there as they would a governor who had gone to Sicily, or to a city or town placed under regular government, and where the laws can be observed in their entirety without fear of ruining everything; and I am greatly injured thereby.

"I ought to be judged as a captain who went from Spain to the Indies to conquer a numerous and warlike people, whose customs and religion are very contrary to ours; who live in rocks and mountains, without fixed settlements, and not like ourselves: and where, by the Divine Will, I have placed under the dominion of the King and Queen, our Sovereigns, a second world, through which Spain, which was reckoned a poor country, has become the richest.

"I ought to be judged as a captain who for such a long time up to this day has borne arms without laying them aside for an hour, and by gentlemen adventurers and by custom, and not by letters, unless they were from Greeks or Romans or others of modern times of whom there are so many and such noble examples in Spain; or otherwise I receive great injury, because in the Indies there is neither town nor settlement.

"The gate to the gold and pearls is now open, and plenty of everything—precious stones, spices and a thousand other things—may be surely expected, and never could a worse misfortune befall me: for by the name of our Lord the first voyage would yield them just as much as would the traffic of Arabia Felix as far as Mecca, as I wrote to their Highnesses by Antonio de Tomes in my reply respecting the repartition of the sea and land with the Portuguese; and afterwards it would equal that of Calicut, as I told them and put in writing at the monastery of the Mejorada.

"The news of the gold that I said I would give is, that on the day of the Nativity, while I was much tormented, being harassed by wicked Christians and by Indians, and when I was on the point of giving up everything, and if possible escaping from life, our Lord miraculously comforted me and said, 'Fear not violence, I will provide for all things: the seven years of the term of the gold have not elapsed, and in that and in everything else I will afford thee a remedy.'

"On that day I learned that there were eighty leagues of land with mines at every point thereof. The opinion now is that it is all one. Some have collected a hundred and twenty castellanos in one day, and others ninety, and even the number of two hundred and fifty has been reached. From fifty to seventy, and in many more cases from fifteen to fifty, is considered a good day's work, and many carry it on. The usual quantity is from six to twelve, and any one obtaining less than this is not satisfied. It seems to me that these mines are like others, and do not yield equally every day. The mines are new, and so are the workers: it is the opinion of everybody that even if all Castile were to go there, every individual, however inexpert he might be, would not obtain less than one or two castellanos daily, and now it is only commencing. It is true that they keep Indians, but the business is in the hands of the Christians. Behold what discernment Bobadilla had, when he gave up everything for nothing, and four millions of tenths, without any reason or even being requested, and without first notifying it to their Highnesses. And this is not the only loss.

"I know that my errors have not been committed with the intention of doing evil, and I believe that their Highnesses regard the matter just as I state it: and I know and see that they deal mercifully even with those who maliciously act to their disservice. I believe and consider it very certain that their clemency will be both greater and more abundant towards me, for I fell therein through ignorance and the force of circumstances, as they will know fully hereafter; and I indeed am their creature, and they will look upon my services, and will acknowledge day by day that they are much profited. They will place everything in the balance, even as Holy Scripture tells us good and evil will be at the day of judgment.

"If, however, they command that another person do judge me, which I cannot believe, and that it be by inquisition in the Indies, I very humbly beseech them to send thither two conscientious and honourable persons at my expense, who I believe will easily, now that gold is discovered, find five marks in four hours. In either case it is needful for them to provide for this matter.

"The Commander on his arrival at San Domingo took up his abode in my house, and just as he found it so he appropriated everything to himself. Well and good; perhaps he was in want of it. A pirate never acted thus towards a merchant. About my papers I have a greater grievance, for he has so completely deprived me of them that I have never been able to obtain a single one from him; and those that would have been most useful in my exculpation are precisely those which he has kept most concealed. Behold the just and honest inquisitor! Whatever he may have done, they tell me that there has been an end to justice, except in an arbitrary form. God, our Lord, is present with His strength and wisdom, as of old, and always punishes in the end, especially ingratitude and injuries."

We must keep in mind the circumstances in which this letter was written if we are to judge it and the writer wisely. It is a sad example of querulous complaint, in which everything but the writer's personal point of view is ignored. No one indeed is more terrible in this world than the Man with a Grievance. How rarely will human nature in such circumstances retire into the stronghold of silence! Columbus is asking for pity; but as we read his letter we incline to pity him on grounds quite different from those which he represented. He complains that the people he was sent to govern have waged war against him as against a Moor; he complains of Ojeda and of Vincenti Yanez Pinzon; of Adrian de Moxeca, and of every other person whom it was his business to govern and hold in restraint. He complains of the colonists—the very people, some of them, whom he himself took and impressed from the gaols and purlieus of Cadiz; and then he mingles pious talk about Saint Peter and Daniel in the den of lions with notes on the current price of little girls and big lumps of gold like the eggs of geese, hens, and pullets. He complains that he is judged as a man would be judged who had been sent out to govern a ready-made colony, and represents instead that he went out to conquer a numerous and warlike people "whose custom and religion are very contrary to ours, and who lived in rocks and mountains"; forgetting that when it suited him for different purposes he described the natives as so peaceable and unwarlike that a thousand of them would not stand against one Christian, and that in any case he was sent out to create a constitution and not merely to administer one. Very sore indeed is Christopher as he reveals himself in this letter, appealing now to his correspondent, now to the King and Queen, now to that God who is always on the side of the complainant. "God our Lord is present with His strength and wisdom, as of old, and always punishes in the end, especially ingratitude and injuries." Not boastfulness and weakness, let us hope, or our poor Admiral will come off badly.

CHAPTER II

CRISIS IN THE ADMIRAL'S LIFE

Columbus was not far wrong in his estimate of the effect likely to be produced by his manacles, and when the ships of Villegio arrived at Cadiz in October, the spectacle of an Admiral in chains produced a degree of commiseration which must have exceeded his highest hopes. He was now in his fiftieth year and of an extremely venerable appearance, his kindling eye looking forth from under brows of white, his hair and beard snow-white, his face lined and spiritualised with suffering and sorrow. It must be remembered that before the Spanish people he had always appeared in more or less state. They had not that intimacy with him, an intimacy which perhaps brought contempt, which the people in Espanola enjoyed; and in Spain, therefore, the contrast between his former grandeur and this condition of shame and degradation was the more striking. It was a fact that the people of Spain could not neglect. It touched their sense of the dramatic and picturesque, touched their hearts also perhaps—hearts quick to burn, quick to forget. They had forgotten him before, now they burned with indignation at the picture of this venerable and much-suffering man arriving in disgrace.

His letter to Dofia Juana, hastily despatched by him, probably through the office of some friendly soul on board, immediately on his arrival at Cadiz, was the first news from the ship received by the King and Queen, and naturally it caused them a shock of surprise. It was followed by the despatches from Bobadilla and by a letter from the Alcalde of Cadiz announcing that Columbus and his brothers were in his custody awaiting the royal orders. Perhaps Ferdinand and Isabella had already repented their drastic action and had entertained some misgivings as to its results; but it is more probable that they had put it out of their heads altogether, and that their hasty action now was prompted as much by the shock of being recalled to a consciousness of the troubled state of affairs in the New World as by any real regret for what they had done. Moreover they had sent out Bobadilla to quiet things down; and the first result of it was that Spain was ringing with the scandal of the Admiral's treatment. In that Spanish world, unsteadfast and unstable, when one end of the see-saw was up the other must be down; and it was Columbus who now found himself high up in the heavens of favour, and Bobadilla who was seated in the dust. Equipoise any kind was apparently a thing impossible; if one man was right the other man must be wrong; no excuses for Bobadilla; every excuse for the Admiral.

The first official act, therefore, was an order for the immediate release of the Admiral and his brothers, followed by an invitation for him to proceed without delay to the Court at Granada, and an order for the immediate payment to him of the sum of 2000 ducats [perhaps $250,000 in the year 2000 D.W.] this last no ungenerous gift to a Viceroy whose pearl accounts were in something less than order. Perhaps Columbus had cherished the idea of appearing dramatically before the very Court in his rags and chains; but the cordiality of their letter as well as the gift of money made this impossible. Instead, not being a man to do things by halves, he equipped himself in his richest and most splendid garments, got together the requisite number of squires and pages, and duly presented himself at Granada in his full dignity. The meeting was an affecting one, touched with a humanity which has survived the intervening centuries, as a touch of true humanity will when details of mere parade and etiquette have long perished. Perhaps the Admiral, inspired with a deep sense of his wrongs, meant to preserve a very stiff and cold demeanour at the beginning of this interview; but when he looked into the kind eyes of Isabella and saw them suffused with tears at the thought of his sorrows all his dignity broke down; the tears came to his own eyes, and he wept there naturally like a child. Ferdinand looking on kind but uncomfortable; Isabella unaffectedly touched and weeping; the Admiral, in spite of his scarlet cloak and golden collar and jewelled sword, in spite of equerries, squires, pages and attendants, sobbing on his knees like a child or an old man-these were the scenes and kindly emotions of this historic moment.

The tears were staunched by kindly royal words and handkerchiefs supplied by attendant pages; sobbings breaking out again, but on the whole soon quieted; King and Queen raising the gouty Christopher from his knees, filling the air with kind words of sympathy, praise, and encouragement; the lonely worn heart, somewhat arid of late, and parched from want of human sympathy, much refreshed by this dew of kindness. The Admiral was soon himself again, and he would not have been himself if upon recovering he had not launched out into what some historians call a "lofty and dignified vindication of his loyalty and zeal." No one, indeed, is better than the Admiral at such lofty and dignified vindications. He goes into the whole matter and sets forth an account of affairs at Espanola from his own point of view; and can even (so high is the thermometer of favour) safely indulge in a little judicious self-depreciation, saying that if he has erred it has not been from want of zeal but from want of experience in dealing with the kind of material he has been set to govern. All this is very human, natural, and understandable; product of that warm emotional atmosphere, bedewed with tears, in which the Admiral finds himself; and it is not long before the King and Queen, also moved to it by the emotional temperature, are expressing their unbroken and unbounded confidence in him and repudiating the acts of Bobadilla, which they declare to have been contrary to their instructions; undertaking also that he shall be immediately dismissed from his post. Poor Bobadilla is not here in the warm emotional atmosphere; he had his turn of it six months ago, when no powers were too high or too delicate to be entrusted to him; he is out in the cold at the other end of the see-saw, which has let him down to the ground with a somewhat sudden thump.

Columbus, relying on the influence of these emotions, made bold to ask that his property in the island should be restored to him, which was immediately granted; and also to request that he should be reinstated in his office of Viceroy and allowed to return at once in triumph to Espanola. But emotions are unstable things; they present a yielding surface which will give to any extent, but which, when it has hardened again after the tears have evaporated, is often found to be in much the same condition as before. At first promises were made that the whole matter should be fully gone into; but when it came to cold fact, Ferdinand was obliged to recognise that this whole business of discovery and colonisation had become a very different thing to what it had been when Columbus was the only discoverer; and he was obviously of opinion that, as Columbus's office had once been conveniently withdrawn from him, it would only be disastrous to reinstate him in it. Of course he did not say so at once; but reasons were given for judicious delay in the Admiral's reappointment. It was represented to him that the colony, being in an extremely unsettled state, should be given a short period of rest, and also that it would be as well for him to wait until the people who had given him so much trouble in the island could be quietly and gradually removed. Two years was the time mentioned as suitable for an interregnum, and it is probable that it was the intention of Isabella, although not of Ferdinand, to restore Columbus to his office at the end of that time.

In the meantime it became necessary to appoint some one to supersede Bobadilla; for the news that arrived periodically from Espanola during the year showed that he had entirely failed in his task of reducing the island to order. For the wholesome if unequal rigours of Columbus Bobadilla had substituted laxness and indulgence, with the result that the whole colony was rapidly reduced to a state of the wildest disorder. Vice and cruelty were rampant; in fact the barbarities practised upon the natives were so scandalous that even Spanish opinion, which was never very sympathetic to heathen suffering, was thoroughly shocked and alarmed. The Sovereigns therefore appointed Nicholas de Ovando to go out and take over the command, with instructions to use very drastic means for bringing the colony to order. How he did it we shall presently see; in the meantime all that was known of him (the man not having been tried yet) was that he was a poor knight of Calatrava, a man respected in royal circles for the performance of minor official duties, but no very popular favourite; honest according to his lights—lights turned rather low and dim, as was often the case in those days. A narrow-minded man also, without sympathy or imagination, capable of cruelty; a tough, stiff-necked stock of a man, fit to deal with Bobadilla perhaps, but hardly fit to deal with the colony. Spain in those days was not a nursery of administration. Of all the people who were sent out successively to govern Espanola and supersede one another, the only one who really seems to have had the necessary natural ability, had he but been given the power, was Bartholomew Columbus; but unfortunately things were in such a state that the very name of Columbus was enough to bar a man from acceptance as a governor of Espanola.

It was not for any lack of powers and equipment that this procession of governors failed in their duties. We have seen with what authority Bobadilia had been entrusted; and Ovando had even greater advantages. The instructions he received showed that the needs of the new colonies were understood by Ferdinand and Isabella, if by no one else. Ovando was not merely appointed Governor of Espanola but of the whole of the new territory discovered in the west, his seat of government being San Domingo. He was given the necessary free hand in the matters of punishment, confiscation, and allotment of lands. He was to revoke the orders which had been made by Bobadilla reducing the proportion of gold payable to the Crown, and was empowered to take over one-third of the. gold that was stored on the island, and one-half of what might be found in the future. The Crown was to have a monopoly of all trade, and ordinary supplies were only to be procured through the Crown agent. On the other hand, the natives were to be released from slavery, and although forced to work in the mines, were to be paid for their labour —a distinction which in the working out did not produce much difference. A body of Franciscan monks accompanied Ovando for the purpose of tackling the religious question with the necessary energy; and every regulation that the kind heart of Isabella could think of was made for the happiness and contentment of the Indians.

Unhappily the real mischief had already been done. The natives, who had never been accustomed to hard and regular work under the conditions of commerce and greed, but had only toiled for the satisfaction of their own simple wants, were suffering cruelly under the hard labour in the mines, and the severe driving of their Spanish masters. Under these unnatural conditions the native population was rapidly dying off, and there was some likelihood that there would soon be a scarcity of native labour. These were the circumstances in which the idea of importing black African labour to the New World was first conceived—a plan which was destined to have results so tremendous that we have probably not yet seen their full and ghastly development. There were a great number of African negro slaves at that time in Spain; a whole generation of them had been born in slavery in Spain itself; and this generation was bodily imported to Espanola to relieve and assist the native labour.

These preparations were not made all at once; and it was more than a year after the return of Columbus before Ovando was ready to sail. In the meantime Columbus was living in Granada, and looking on with no very satisfied eye at the plans which were being made to supersede him, and about which he was probably not very much consulted; feeling very sore indeed, and dividing his attention between the nursing of his grievances and other even less wholesome occupations. There was any amount of smiling kindness for him at Court, but very little of the satisfaction that his vanity and ambition craved; and in the absence of practical employment he fell back on visionary speculations. He made great friends at this time with a monk named Gaspar Gorricio, with whose assistance he began to make some kind of a study of such utterances of the Prophets and the Fathers as he conceived to have a bearing on his own career.

Columbus was in fact in a very queer way at this time; and what with his readings and his meditatings and his grievances, and his visits to his monkish friend in the convent of Las Cuevas, he fell into a kind of intellectual stupor, of which the work called 'Libro de las Profecias,' or Book of the Prophecies, in which he wrote down such considerations as occurred to him in his stupor, was the result. The manuscript of this work is in existence, although no human being has ever ventured to reprint the whole of it; and we would willingly abstain from mentioning it here if it were not an undeniable act of Columbus's life. The Admiral, fallen into theological stupor, puts down certain figures upon paper; discovers that St. Augustine said that the world would only last for 7000 years; finds that some other genius had calculated that before the birth of Christ it had existed for 5343 years and 318 days; adds 1501 years from the birth of Christ to his own time; adds up, and finds that the total is 6844 years; subtracts, and discovers that this earthly globe can only last 155 years longer. He remembers also that, still according to the Prophets, certain things must happen before the end of the world; Holy Sepulchre restored to Christianity, heathen converted, second coming of Christ; and decides that he himself is the man appointed by God and promised by the Prophets to perform these works. Good Heavens! in what an entirely dark and sordid stupor is our Christopher now sunk—a veritable slough and quag of stupor out of which, if he does not manage to flounder himself, no human hand can pull him.

But amid his wallowings in this slough of stupor, when all else, in him had been well-nigh submerged by it, two dim lights were preserved towards which, although foundered up to the chin, he began to struggle; and by superhuman efforts did at last extricate himself from the theological stupor and get himself blown clean again by the salt winds before he died. One light was his religion; not to be confounded with theological stupor, but quite separate from it in my belief; a certain steadfast and consuming faith in a Power that could see and understand and guide him to the accomplishment of his purpose. This faith had been too often a good friend and help to Christopher for him to forget it very long, even while he was staggering in the quag with Isaiah, Jeremiah, and the Fathers; and gradually, as I say, he worked himself out into the region of activity again. First, thinking it a pity that his flounderings in the slough should be entirely wasted, he had a copy of his precious theological work made and presented it to the Sovereigns, with a letter urging them (since he himself was unable to do it) to undertake a crusade for the recovery of the Holy Sepulchre—not an altogether wild proposal in those days. But Ferdinand had other uses for his men and his money, and contented himself with despatching Peter Martyr on a pacific mission to the Grand Soldan of Egypt.

The other light left unquenched in Columbus led him back to the firm ground of maritime enterprise; he began to long for the sea again, and for a chance of doing something to restore his reputation. An infinitely better and more wholesome frame of mind this; by all means let him mend his reputation by achievement, instead of by writing books in a theological trance or stupor, and attempting to prove that he was chosen by the Almighty. He now addressed himself to the better task of getting himself chosen by men to do something which should raise him again in their esteem.

His maritime ambition was no doubt stimulated at this time by witnessing the departure of Ovando, in February 1502, with a fleet of thirty-five ships and a company of 2500 people. It was not in the Admiral's nature to look on without envy at an equipment the like of which he himself had never been provided with, and he did not restrain his sarcasms at its pomp and grandeur, nor at the ease with which men could follow a road which had once been pointed out to them. Ovando had a great body-guard such as Columbus had never had; and he also carried with him a great number of picked married men with their families, all with knowledge of some trade or craft, whose presence in the colony would be a guarantee of permanence and steadiness. He perhaps remembered his own crowd of ruffians and gaol-birds, and realised the bitterness of his own mistakes. It was a very painful moment for him, and he was only partially reconciled to it by the issue of a royal order to Ovando under which he was required to see to the restoration of the Admiral's property. If it had been devoted to public purposes it was to be repaid him from the royal funds; but if it had been merely distributed among the colonists Bobadilla was to be made responsible for it. The Admiral was also allowed to send out an agent to represent him and look after his interests; and he appointed Alonso de Carvajal to this office.

Ovando once gone, the Admiral could turn again to his own affairs. It is true there were rumours that the whole fleet had perished, for it encountered a gale very soon after leaving Cadiz, and a great quantity of the deck hamper was thrown overboard and was washed on the shores of Spain; and the Sovereigns were so bitterly distressed that, as it is said, they shut themselves up for eight days. News eventually came, however, that only one ship had been lost and that the rest had proceeded safely to San Domingo. Columbus, much recovered in body and mind, now began to apply for a fleet for himself. He had heard of the discovery by the Portuguese of the southern route to India; no doubt he had heard also much gossip of the results of the many private voyages of discovery that were sailing from Spain at this time; and he began to think seriously about his own discoveries and the way in which they might best be extended. He thought much of his voyage to the west of Trinidad and of the strange pent-up seas and currents that he had discovered there. He remembered the continual westward trend of the current, and how all the islands in that sea had their greatest length east and west, as though their shores had been worn into that shape by the constant flowing of the current; and it was not an unnatural conclusion for him to suppose that there was a channel far to the west through which these seas poured and which would lead him to the Golden Chersonesus. He put away from him that nightmare madness that he transacted on the coast of Cuba. He knew very well that he had not yet found the Golden Chersonesus and the road to India; but he became convinced that the western current would lead him there if only he followed it long enough. There was nothing insane about this theory; it was in fact a very well-observed and well-reasoned argument; and the fact that it happened to be entirely wrong is no reflection on the Admiral's judgment. The great Atlantic currents at that time had not been studied; and how could he know that the western stream of water was the northern half of a great ocean current which sweeps through the Caribbean Sea, into and round the Gulf of Mexico, and flows out northward past Florida in the Gulf Stream?

His applications for a fleet were favourably received by the King and Queen, but much frowned upon by certain high officials of the Court. They were beginning to regard Columbus as a dangerous adventurer who, although he happened to have discovered the western islands, had brought the Spanish colony there to a dreadful state of disorder; and had also, they alleged, proved himself rather less than trustworthy in matters of treasure. Still in the summer days of 1501 he was making himself very troublesome at Court with constant petitions and letters about his rights and privileges; and Ferdinand was far from unwilling to adopt a plan by which they would at least get rid of him and keep him safely occupied at the other side of the world at the cost of a few caravels. There was, besides, always an element of uncertainty. His voyage might come to nothing, but on the other hand the Admiral was no novice at this game of discovery, and one could not tell but that something big might come of it. After some consideration permission was given to him to fit out a fleet of four ships, and he proceeded to Seville in the autumn of 1501 to get his little fleet ready. Bartholomew was to come with him, and his son Ferdinand also, who seems to have much endeared himself to the Admiral in these dark days, and who would surely be a great comfort to him on the voyage. Beatriz Enriquez seems to have passed out of his life; certainly he was not living with her either now or on his last visit to Spain; one way or another, that business is at an end for him. Perhaps poor Beatriz, seeing her son in such a high place at Court, has effaced herself for his sake; perhaps the appointment was given on condition of such effacement; we do not know.

Columbus was in no hurry over his preparations. In the midst of them he found time to collect a whole series of documents relating to his titles and dignities, which he had copied and made into a great book which he called his "Book of Privileges," and the copies of which were duly attested before a notary at Seville on January 5, 1502. He wrote many letters to various friends of his, chiefly in relation to these privileges; not interesting or illuminating letters to us, although very important to busy Christopher when he wrote them. Here is one written to Nicolo Oderigo, a Genoese Ambassador who came to Spain on a brief mission in the spring of 1502, and who, with certain other residents in Spain, is said to have helped Columbus in his preparations for his fourth voyage:

"Sir,—The loneliness in which you have left us cannot be described. I gave the book containing my writings to Francisco de Rivarol that he may send it to you with another copy of letters containing instructions. I beg you to be so kind as to write Don Diego in regard to the place of security in which you put them. Duplicates of everything will be completed and sent to you in the same manner and by the same Francisco. Among them you will find a new document. Their Highnesses promised to give all that belongs to me and to place Don Diego in possession of everything, as you will see. I wrote to Senor Juan Luis and to Sefora Catalina. The letter accompanies this one. I am ready to start in the name of the Holy Trinity as soon as the weather is good. I am well provided with everything. If Jeronimo de Santi

Esteban is coming, he must await me and not embarrass himself with anything, for they will take away from him all they can and silently leave him. Let him come here and the King and the Queen will receive him until I come. May our Lord have you in His holy keeping.

"Done at Seville, March 21, 1502.
"At your command.

.S.

.S.A.S.

Xpo FERENS."

His delays were not pleasing to Ferdinand, who wanted to get rid of him, and he was invited to hurry his departure; but he still continued to go deliberately about his affairs, which he tried to put in order as far as he was able, since he thought it not unlikely that he might never see Spain again. Thinking thus of his worldly duties, and his thoughts turning to his native Genoa, it occurred to him to make some benefaction out of the riches that were coming to him by which his name might be remembered and held in honour there. This was a piece of practical kindness the record of which is most precious to us; for it shows the Admiral in a truer and more human light than he often allowed to shine upon him. The tone of the letter is nothing; he could not forbear letting the people of Genoa see how great he was. The devotion of his legacy to the reduction of the tax on simple provisions was a genuine charity, much to be appreciated by the dwellers in the Vico Dritto di Ponticello, where wine and provision shops were so very necessary to life. The letter was written to the Directors of the famous Bank of Saint George at Genoa.

"VERY NOBLE LORDS,—Although my body is here, my heart is continually yonder. Our Lord has granted me the greatest favour he has granted any one since the time of David. The results of my undertaking already shine, and they would make a great light if the obscurity of the Government did not conceal them. I shall go again to the Indies in the name of the Holy Trinity, to return immediately. And as I am mortal, I desire my son Don Diego to give to you each year, for ever, the tenth part of all the income received, in payment of the tax on wheat, wine, and other provisions. If this tenth amounts to anything, receive it, and if not, receive my will for the deed. I beg you as a favour to have this son of mine in your charge. Nicolo de Oderigo knows more about

my affairs than I myself. I have sent him the copy of my privileges
and letters, that he may place them in safe keeping. I would be
glad if you could see them. The King and the Queen, my Lords, now
wish to honour me more than ever. May the Holy Trinity guard your
noble persons, and increase the importance of your very magnificent
office.

"Done in Seville, April a, 1502.

"The High-Admiral of the Ocean-Sea and Viceroy and Governor-General
of the islands and mainland of Asia and the Indies, belonging to the
King and Queen, my Lords, and the Captain-General of the Sea, and a
Member of their Council.

.S.

.S.A.S.

X M Y

Xpo FERENS."

Columbus was anxious to touch at Espanola on his voyage to the West; but he was
expressly forbidden to do so, as it was known that his presence there could not make
for anything but confusion; he was to be permitted, however, to touch there on his
return journey. The Great Khan was not out of his mind yet; much in it apparently,
for he took an Arabian interpreter with him so that he could converse with that
monarch. In fact he did not hesitate to announce that very big results indeed were to
come of this voyage of his; among other things he expected to circumnavigate the
globe, and made no secret of his expectation. In the meantime he was expected to
find some pearls in order to pay for the equipment of his fleet; and in consideration of
what had happened to the last lot of pearls collected by him, an agent named Diego
de Porras was sent along with him to keep an account of the gold and precious stones
which might be discovered. Special instructions were issued to Columbus about the
disposal of these commodities. He does not seem to have minded these somewhat
humiliating precautions; he had a way of rising above petty indignities and refusing
to recognise them which must have been of great assistance to his self-respect in
certain troubled moments in his life.

His delays, however, were so many that in March 1502 the Sovereigns were obliged
to order him to depart without any more waiting. Poor Christopher, who once had to
sue for the means with which to go, whose departures were once the occasion of so
much state and ceremony, has now to be hustled forth and asked to go away. Still he

does not seem to mind; once more, as of old, his gaze is fixed beyond the horizon and his mind is filled with one idea. They may not think much of him in Spain now, but they will when he comes back; and he can afford to wait. Completing his preparations without undignified haste he despatched Bartholomew with his four little vessels from Seville to Cadiz, where the Admiral was to join them. He took farewell of his son Diego and of his brother James; good friendly James, who had done his best in a difficult position, but had seen quite enough of the wild life of the seas and was now settled in Seville studying hard for the Church. It had always been his ambition, poor James; and, studying hard in Seville, he did in time duly enter the sacred pale and become a priest—by which we may see that if our ambitions are only modest enough we may in time encompass them. Sometimes I think that James, enveloped in priestly vestments, nodding in the sanctuary, lulled by the muttering murmur of the psalms or dozing through a long credo, may have thought himself back amid the brilliant sunshine and strange perfumes of Espanola; and from a dream of some nymph hiding in the sweet groves of the Vega may have awakened with a sigh to the strident Alleluias of his brother priests. At any rate, farewell to James, safely seated beneath the Gospel light, and continuing to sit there until, in the year 1515, death interrupts him. We are not any more concerned with James in his priestly shelter, but with those elder brothers of his who are making ready again to face the sun and the surges.

Columbus's ships were on the point of sailing when word came that the Moors were besieging a Portuguese post on the coast of Morocco, and, as civility was now the order of the day between Spain and Portugal, the Admiral was instructed to call on his way there and afford some relief. This he did, sailing from Cadiz on the 9th or 10th of May to Ercilla on the Morocco coast, where he anchored on the 13th. But the Moors had all departed and the siege was over; so Columbus, having sent Bartholomew and some of his officers ashore on a civil visit, which was duly returned, set out the same day on his last voyage.

CHAPTER III

THE LAST VOYAGE

The four ships that made up the Admiral's fleet on his fourth and last voyage were all small caravels, the largest only of seventy tons and the smallest only of fifty. Columbus chose for his flagship the Capitana, seventy tons, appointing Diego Tristan to be his captain. The next best ship was the Santiago de Palos under the command of Francisco Porras; Porras and his brother Diego having been more or less foisted on to Columbus by Morales, the Royal Treasurer, who wished to find berths for these two brothers-in-law of his. We shall hear more of the Porras brothers. The third ship was the Gallega, sixty tons, a very bad sailer indeed, and on that account entrusted to Bartholomew Columbus, whose skill in navigation, it was hoped, might make up for her bad sailing qualities. Bartholomew had, to tell the truth, had quite enough of the New World, but he was too loyal to Christopher to let him go alone, knowing as he did his precarious state of health and his tendency to despondency. The captain of the Gallega was Pedro de Terreros, who had sailed with the Admiral as steward on all his other voyages and was now promoted to a command. The fourth ship was called the Vizcaina, fifty tons, and was commanded by Bartolome Fieschi, a friend of Columbus's from Genoa, and a very sound, honourable man. There were altogether 143 souls on board the four caravels.

The fleet as usual made the Canary Islands, where they arrived on the 20th of May, and stopped for five days taking in wood and water and fresh provisions. Columbus was himself again—always more himself at sea than anywhere else; he was following a now familiar road that had no difficulties or dangers for him; and there is no record of the voyage out except that it was quick and prosperous, with the trade wind blowing so steadily that from the time they left the Canaries until they made land twenty days later they had hardly to touch a sheet or a halliard. The first land they made was the island of Martinique, where wood and water were taken in and the men sent ashore to wash their linen. To young Ferdinand, but fourteen years old, this voyage was like a fairy tale come true, and his delight in everything that he saw must have added greatly to Christopher's pleasure and interest in the voyage. They only stayed a few days at Martinique and then sailed westward along the chain of islands until they came to Porto Rico, where they put in to the sunny harbour which they had discovered on a former voyage.

It was at this point that Columbus determined, contrary to his precise orders, to stand across to Espanola. The place attracted him like a magnet; he could not keep away from it; and although he had a good enough excuse for touching there, it is probable that his real reason was a very natural curiosity to see how things were faring with his old enemy Bobadilla. The excuse was that the Gallega, Bartholomew's ship, was so unseaworthy as to be a drag on the progress of the rest of the fleet and a danger to her own crew. In the slightest sea-way she rolled almost gunwale under, and would not carry her sail; and Columbus's plan was to exchange her for a vessel out of the great fleet which he knew had by this time reached Espanola and discharged its passengers.

He arrived off the harbour of San Domingo on the 29th of June in very threatening weather, and immediately sent Pedro de Terreros ashore with a message to Ovando, asking to be allowed to purchase or exchange one of the vessels that were riding in the harbour, and also leave to shelter his own vessels there during the hurricane which he believed to be approaching. A message came back that he was neither permitted to buy a ship nor to enter the harbour; warning him off from San Domingo, in fact.

With this unfavourable message Terreros also brought back the news of the island. Ovando had been in San Domingo since the 15th of April, and had found the island in a shocking state, the Spanish population having to a man devoted itself to idleness, profligacy, and slave-driving. The only thing that had prospered was the gold-mining; for owing to the licence that Bobadilla had given to the Spaniards to employ native labour to an unlimited extent there had been an immense amount of gold taken from the mines. But in no other respect had island affairs prospered, and Ovando immediately began the usual investigation. The fickle Spaniards, always unfaithful to whoever was in authority over them, were by this time tired of Bobadilla, in spite of his leniency, and they hailed the coming of Ovando and his numerous equipment with enthusiasm. Bobadilla had also by this time, we may suppose, had enough of the joys of office; at any rate he showed no resentment at the coming of the new Governor, and handed over the island with due ceremony. The result of the investigation of Ovando, however, was to discover a state of things requiring exemplary treatment; friend Roldan was arrested, with several of his allies, and put on board one of the ships to be sent back to Spain for trial. The cacique Guarionex, who had been languishing in San Domingo in chains for a long time, was also embarked on one of the returning ships; and about eighteen hundred-weights of gold which had been collected were also stowed into cases and embarked. Among this gold there was a nugget weighing 35 lbs. which had been found by a native woman in a river, and which Ovando was sending home as a personal offering to his Sovereigns; and some further 40 lbs. of gold belonging to Columbus, which Carvajal had recovered and placed in a caravel to be taken to Spain for the Admiral. The ships were all ready to sail, and were anchored off the mouth of the river when Columbus arrived in San Domingo.

When he found that he was not to be allowed to enter the harbour himself Columbus sent a message to Ovando warning him that a hurricane was coming on, and begging him to take measures for the safety of his large fleet. This, however, was not done, and the fleet put to sea that evening. It had only got so far as the eastern end of Espanola when the hurricane, as predicted by Columbus, duly came down in the manner of West Indian hurricanes, a solid wall of wind and an advancing wave of the sea which submerged everything in its path. Columbus's little fleet, finding shelter denied them, had moved a little way along the coast, the Admiral standing close in shore, the others working to the south for sea-room; and although they survived the hurricane they were scattered, and only met several days later, in an extremely battered condition, at the westerly end of the island. But the large home-going fleet had not survived. The hurricane, which was probably from the north-east, struck them just as they lost the lee of the island, and many of them, including the ships with the treasure of gold and the caravels bearing Roldan, Bobadilla, and Guarionex, all went down at once and were never seen or heard of again. Other ships survived for a little while only to founder in the end; a few, much shattered, crept back to the shelter of San Domingo; but only one, it is said, survived the hurricane so well as to be able to proceed to Spain; and that was the one which carried Carvajal and Columbus's little property of gold. The Admiral's luck again; or the intervention of the Holy Trinity—whichever you like.

After the shattering experience of the storm, Columbus, although he did not return to San Domingo, remained for some time on the coast of Espanola repairing his ships and resting his exhausted crews. There were threatenings of another storm which delayed them still further, and it was not until the middle of July that the Admiral was able to depart on the real purpose of his voyage. His object was to strike the mainland far to the westward of the Gulf of Paria, and so by following it back eastward to find the passage which he believed to exist. But the winds and currents were very baffling; he was four days out of sight of land after touching at an island north of Jamaica; and finally, in some bewilderment, he altered his course more and more northerly until he found his whereabouts by coming in sight of the archipelago off the south-western end of Cuba which he had called the Gardens. From here he took a departure south-west, and on the 30th of July came in sight of a small island off the northern coast of Honduras which he called Isla de Pinos, and from which he could see the hills of the mainland. At this island he found a canoe of immense size with a sort of house or caboose built amidships, in which was established a cacique with his family and dependents; and the people in the canoe showed signs of more advanced civilisation than any seen by Columbus before in these waters. They wore clothing, they had copper hatchets, and bells, and palm-wood swords in the edges of which were set sharp blades of flint. They had a fermented liquor, a kind of maize beer which looked like English ale; they had some kind of money or medium of exchange also, and they told the Admiral that there was land to the west where all these things existed and many more. It is strange and almost inexplicable that he did not follow this trail to the westward; if he had done so he would have discovered Mexico. But one thing at a time always occupied him to the exclusion of everything else; his thoughts were now turned to the eastward, where he supposed the Straits were; and the significance of this canoe full of natives was lost upon him.

They crossed over to the mainland of Honduras on August 15th, Bartholomew landing and attending mass on the beach as the Admiral himself was too ill to go ashore. Three days later the cross and banner of Castile were duly erected on the shores of the Rio Tinto and the country was formally annexed. The natives were friendly, and supplied the ships with provisions; but they were very black and ugly, and Columbus readily believed the assertion of his native guide that they were cannibals. They continued their course to the eastward, but as the gulf narrowed the force of the west-going current was felt more severely. Columbus, believing that the strait which he sought lay to the eastward, laboured against the current, and his difficulties were increased by the bad weather which he now encountered. There were squalls and hurricanes, tempests and cross-currents that knocked his frail ships about and almost swamped them. Anchors and gear were lost, the sails were torn out of the bolt-ropes, timbers were strained; and for six weeks this state of affairs went on to an accompaniment of thunder and lightning which added to the terror and discomfort of the mariners.

This was in August and the first half of September—six weeks of the worst weather that Columbus had ever experienced. It was the more unfortunate that his illness made it impossible for him to get actively about the ship; and he had to have a small cabin or tent rigged up on deck, in which he could lie and direct the navigation. It is bad enough to be as ill as he was in a comfortable bed ashore; it is a thousand times worse amid the discomforts of a small boat at sea; but what must it have been thus to have one's sick-bed on the deck of a cockle-shell which was being buffeted and smashed in unknown seas, and to have to think and act not for oneself alone but for the whole of a suffering little fleet! No wonder the Admiral's distress of mind was great; but oddly enough his anxieties, as he recorded them in a letter, were not so much on his own account as on behalf of others. The terrified seamen making vows to the Virgin and promises of pilgrimages between their mad rushes to the sheets and furious clinging and hauling; his son Ferdinand, who was only fourteen, but who had to endure the same pain and fatigue as the rest of them, and who was enduring it with such pluck that "it was as if he had been at sea eighty years"; the dangers of Bartholomew, who had not wanted to come on this voyage at all, but was now in the thick of it in the worst ship of the squadron, and fighting for his life amid tempests and treacherous seas; Diego at home, likely to be left an orphan and at the mercy of fickle and doubtful friends—these were the chief causes of the Admiral's anxiety. All he said about himself was that "by my misfortune the twenty years of service which I gave with so much fatigue and danger have profited me so little that to-day I have in Castile no roof, and if I wished to dine or sup or sleep I have only the tavern for my last refuge, and for that, most of the time, I would be unable to pay the score." Not cheerful reflections, these, to add to the pangs of acute gout and the consuming anxieties of seamanship under such circumstances. Dreadful to him, these things, but not dreadful to us; for they show us an Admiral restored to his true temper and vocation, something of the old sea hero breaking out in him at last through all these misfortunes, like the sun through the hurrying clouds of a stormy afternoon.

Forty days of passage through this wilderness of water were endured before the sea-worn mariners, rounding a cape on September 12th, saw stretching before them to the southward a long coast of plain and mountain which they were able to follow with a fair wind. Gradually the sea went down; the current which had opposed them here aided them, and they were able to recover a little from the terrible strain of the last six weeks. The cape was called by Columbus 'Gracios de Dios'; and on the 16th of September they landed at the entrance to a river to take in water. The boat which was sent ashore, however, capsized on the sandy bar of the entrance, two men being drowned, and the river was given the name of Rio de Desastre. They found a better anchorage, where they rested for ten days, overhauled their stores, and had some intercourse with the natives and exploration on shore. Some incidents occurred which can best be described in the Admiral's own language as he recorded them in his letter to the Sovereigns.

" . . When I reached there, they immediately sent me two young girls dressed in rich garments. The older one might not have been more than eleven years of age and the other seven; both with so much experience, so much manner, and so much appearance as would have been sufficient if they had been public women for twenty years. They bore with them magic powder and other things belonging to their art. When they arrived I gave orders that they should be adorned with our things and sent them immediately ashore. There I saw a tomb within the mountain as large as a house and finely worked with great artifice, and a corpse stood thereon uncovered, and, looking within it, it seemed as if he stood upright. Of the other arts they told me that there was excellence. Great and little animals are there in quantities, and very different from ours; among which I saw boars of frightful form so that a dog of the Irish breed dared not face them. With a cross-bow I had wounded an animal which exactly resembles a baboon only that it was much larger and has a face like a human being. I had pierced it with an arrow from one side to the other, entering in the breast and going out near the tail, and because it was very ferocious I cut off one of the fore feet which rather seemed to be a hand, and one of the hind feet. The boars seeing this commenced to set up their bristles and fled with great fear, seeing the blood of the other animal. When I saw this I caused to be thrown them the 'uegare,'—[Peccary]—certain animals they call so, where it stood, and approaching him, near as he was to death, and the arrow still sticking in his body, he wound his tail around his snout and held it fast, and with the other hand which remained free, seized him by the neck as an enemy. This act, so magnificent and novel, together with the fine country and hunting of wild beasts, made me write this to your Majesties."

The natives at this anchorage of Cariari were rather suspicious, but Columbus seized two of them to act as guides in his journey further down the coast. Weighing anchor on October 5th he worked along the Costa Rica shore, which here turns to the eastward again, and soon found a tribe of natives who wore large ornaments of gold. They were reluctant to part with the gold, but as usual pointed down the coast and said that there was much more gold there; they even gave a name to the place where the gold could be found—Veragua; and for once this country was found to have a real existence. The fleet anchored there on October 17th, being greeted by defiant blasts of conch shells and splashing of water from the indignant natives. Business was done, however: seventeen gold discs in exchange for three hawks' bells.

Still Columbus went on in pursuit of his geographical chimera; even gold had no power to detain him from the earnest search for this imaginary strait. Here and there along the coast he saw increasing signs of civilisation—once a wall built of mud and stone, which made him think of Cathay again. He now got it into his head that the region he was in was ten days' journey from the Ganges, and that it was surrounded by water; which if it means anything means that he thought he was on a large island ten days' sail to the eastward of the coast of India. Altogether at sea as to the facts, poor Admiral, but with heart and purpose steadfast and right enough.

They sailed a little farther along the coast, now between narrow islands that were like the streets of Genoa, where the boughs of trees on either hand brushed the shrouds of the ships; now past harbours where there were native fairs and markets, and where natives were to be seen mounted on horses and armed with swords; now by long, lonely stretches of the coast where there was nothing to be seen but the low green shore with the mountains behind and the alligators basking at the river mouths. At last (November 2nd) they arrived at the cape known as Nombre de Dios, which Ojeda had reached some time before in his voyage to the West.

The coast of the mainland had thus been explored from the Bay of Honduras to Brazil, and Columbus was obliged to admit that there was no strait. Having satisfied himself of that he decided to turn back to Veragua, where he had seen the natives smelting gold, in order to make some arrangement for establishing a colony there. The wind, however, which had headed him almost all the way on his easterly voyage, headed him again now and began to blow steadily from the west. He started on his return journey on the 5th of December, and immediately fell into almost worse troubles than he had been in before. The wood of the ships had been bored through and through by seaworms, so that they leaked very badly; the crews were sick, provisions were spoilt, biscuits rotten. Young Ferdinand Columbus, if he did not actually make notes of this voyage at the time, preserved a very lively recollection of it, and it is to his Historie, which in its earlier passages is of doubtful authenticity, that we owe some of the most human touches of description relating to this voyage. Any passage in his work relating to food or animals at this time has the true ring of boyish interest and observation, and is in sharp contrast to the second-hand and artificial tone of the earlier chapters of his book. About the incident of the howling monkey, which the Admiral's Irish hound would not face, Ferdinand remarks that it "frighted a good dog that we had, but frighted one of our wild boars a great deal more"; and as to the condition of the biscuits when they turned westward again, he says that they were "so full of weevils that, as God shall help me, I saw many that stayed till night to eat their sop for fear of seeing them."

After experiencing some terrible weather, in the course of which they had been obliged to catch sharks for food and had once been nearly overwhelmed by a waterspout, they entered a harbour where, in the words of young Ferdinand, "we saw the people living like birds in the tops of the trees, laying sticks across from bough to bough and building their huts upon them; and though we knew not the reason of the custom we guessed that it was done for fear of their enemies, or of the griffins that are in this island." After further experiences of bad weather they made what looked like a suitable harbour on the coast of Veragua, which harbour, as they entered it on the day of the Epiphany (January 9, 1503), they named Belem or Bethlehem. The river in the mouth of which they were anchored, however, was subject to sudden spouts and gushes of water from the hills, one of which occurred on January 24th and nearly swamped the caravels. This spout of water was caused by the rainy season, which had begun in the mountains and presently came down to the coast, where it rained continuously until the 14th of February. They had made friends with the Quibian or chief of the country, and he had offered to conduct them to the place where the gold mines were; so Bartholomew was sent off in the rain with a boat party to find this territory. It turned out afterwards that the cunning Quibian had taken them out of his own country and showed them the gold mined of a neighbouring chief, which were not so rich as his own.

Columbus, left idle in the absence of Bartholomew, listening to the continuous drip and patter of the rain on the leaves and the water, begins to dream again—to dream of gold and geography. Remembers that David left three thousand quintals of gold from the Indies to Solomon for the decoration of the Temple; remembers that Josephus said it came from the Golden Chersonesus; decides that enough gold could never have been got from the mines of Hayna in Espanola; and concludes that the Ophir of Solomon must be here in Veragua and not there in Espanola. It was always here and now with Columbus; and as he moved on his weary sea pilgrimages these mythical lands with their glittering promise moved about with him, like a pillar of fire leading him through the dark night of his quest.

The rain came to an end, however, the sun shone out again, and activity took the place of dreams with Columbus and with his crew. He decided to found a settlement in this place, and to make preparations for seizing and working the gold mines. It was decided to leave a garrison of eighty men, and the business of unloading the necessary arms and provisions and building houses ashore was immediately begun. Hawks' bells and other trifles were widely distributed among the natives, with special toys and delicacies for the Quibian, in order that friendly relations might be established from the beginning; and special regulations were framed to prevent the possibility of any recurrence of the disasters that overtook the settlers of Isabella.

Such are the orderly plans of Columbus; but the Quibian has his plans too, which are found to be of quite a different nature. The Quibian does not like intruders, though he likes their hawks' bells well enough; he is not quite so innocent as poor Guacanagari and the rest of them were; he knows that gold is a thing coveted by people to whom it does not belong, and that trouble follows in its train. Quibian therefore decides that Columbus and his followers shall be exterminated—news of which intention fortunately came to the ears of Columbus in time, Diego Mendez and Rodrigo de Escobar having boldly advanced into the Quibian's village and seen the warlike preparations. Bartholomew, returning from his visit to the gold mines, was informed of this state of affairs. Always quick to strike, Bartholomew immediately started with an armed force, and advanced upon the village so rapidly that the savages were taken by surprise, their headquarters surrounded, and the Quibian and fifty of his warriors captured. Bartholomew triumphantly marched the prisoners back, the Quibian being entrusted to the charge of Juan Sanchez, who was rowing him in a little boat. The Quibian complained that his bonds were hurting him, and foolish Sanchez eased them a little; Quibian, with a quick movement, wriggled overboard and dived to the bottom; came up again somewhere and reached home alive. No one saw him come up, however, and they thought had had been drowned.

Columbus now made ready to depart, and the caravels having been got over the shallow bar, their loading was completed and they were ready to sail. On April 6th Diego Tristan was sent in charge of a boat with a message to Bartholomew, who was to be left in command of the settlement; but when Tristan had rounded the point at the entrance to the river and come in sight of the shore he had an unpleasant surprise; the settlement was being savagely attacked by the resurrected Quibian and his followers. The fight had lasted for three hours, and had been going badly against the Spaniards, when Bartholomew and Diego Mendes rallied a little force round them and, calling to Columbus's Irish dog which had been left with them, made a rush upon the savages and so terrified them that they scattered. Bartholomew with eight of the other Spaniards was wounded, and one was killed; and it was at this point that Tristan's boat arrived at the settlement. Having seen the fight safely over, he went on up the river to get water, although he was warned that it was not safe; and sure enough, at a point a little farther up the river, beyond some low green arm of the shore, he met with a sudden and bloody death. A cloud of yelling savages surrounded his boat hurling javelins and arrows, and only one seaman, who managed to dive into the water and crawl ashore, escaped to bring the evil tidings.

The Spaniards under Bartholomew's command broke into a panic, and taking advantage of his wounded condition they tried to make sail on their caravel and join the ships of Columbus outside; but since the time of the rains the river had so much gone down that she was stuck fast in the sand. They could not even get a boat over the bar, for there was a heavy cross sea breaking on it; and in the meantime here they were, trapped inside this river, the air resounding with dismal blasts of the natives' conch-shells, and the natives themselves dancing round and threatening to rush their position; while the bodies of Tristan and his little crew were to be seen floating down the stream, feasted upon by a screaming cloud of birds. The position of the shore party was desperate, and it was only by the greatest efforts that the wounded

Adelantado managed to rally his crew and get them to remove their little camp to an open place on the shore, where a kind of stockade was made of chests, casks, spars, and the caravel's boat. With this for cover, the Spanish fire-arms, so long as there was ammunition for them, were enough to keep the natives at bay.

Outside the bar, in his anchorage beyond the green wooded point, the Admiral meanwhile was having an anxious time. One supposes the entrance to the river to have been complicated by shoals and patches of broken water extending some considerable distance, so that the Admiral's anchorage would be ten or twelve miles away from the camp ashore, and of course entirely hidden from it. As day after day passed and Diego Tristan did not return, the Admiral's anxiety increased. Among the three caravels that now formed his little squadron there was only one boat remaining, the others, not counting one taken by Tristan and one left with Bartholomew, having all been smashed in the late hurricanes. In the heavy sea that was running on the bar the Admiral dared not risk his last remaining boat; but in the mean time he was cut off from all news of the shore party and deprived of any means of finding out what had happened to Tristan. And presently to these anxieties was added a further disaster. It will be remembered that when the Quibian had been captured fifty natives had been taken with him; and these were confined in the forecastle of the Capitana and covered by a large hatch, on which most of the crew slept at night. But one night the natives collected a heap of big stones from the ballast of the ship, and piled them up to a kind of platform beneath the hatch; some of the strongest of them got upon the platform and set their backs horizontally against the hatch, gave a great heave and, lifted it off. In the confusion that followed, a great many of the prisoners escaped into the sea, and swam ashore; the rest were captured and thrust back under the hatch, which was chained down; but when on the following morning the Spaniards went to attend to this remnant it was found that they had all hanged themselves.

This was a great disaster, since it increased the danger of the garrison ashore, and destroyed all hope of friendship with the natives. There was something terrible and powerful, too, in the spirit of people who could thus to a man make up their minds either to escape or die; and the Admiral must have felt that he was in the presence of strange, powerful elements that were far beyond his control. At any moment, moreover, the wind might change and put him on a lee shore, or force him to seek safety in sea-room; in which case the position of Bartholomew would be a very critical one. It was while things were at this apparent deadlock that a brave fellow, Pedro Ledesma, offered to attempt to swim through the surf if the boat would take him to the edge of it. Brave Pedro, his offer accepted, makes the attempt; plunges into the boiling surf, and with mighty efforts succeeds in reaching the shore; and after an interval is seen by his comrades, who are waiting with their boat swinging on the edge of the surf, to be returning to them; plunges into the sea, comes safely through the surf again, and is safely hauled on board, having accomplished a very real and satisfactory bit of service.

The story he had to tell the Admiral was as we know not a pleasant one —Tristan and his men dead, several of Bartholomew's force, including the Adelantado himself, wounded, and all in a state of panic and fear at the hostile natives. The Spaniards would do nothing to make the little fortress safer, and were bent only on escaping from the place of horror. Some of them were preparing canoes in which to come out to the ships when the sea should go down, as their one small boat was insufficient; and they swore that if the Admiral would not take them they would seize their own caravel and sail out themselves into the unknown sea as soon as they could get her floated over the bar, rather than remain in such a dreadful situation. Columbus was in a very bad way. He could not desert Bartholomew, as that would expose him to the treachery of his own men and the hostility of the savages. He could not reinforce him, except by remaining himself with the whole of his company; and in that case there would be no means of sending the news of his rich discovery to Spain. There was nothing for it, therefore, but to break up the settlement and return some other time with a stronger force sufficient to occupy the country. And even this course had its difficulties; for the weather continued bad, the wind was blowing on to the shore, the sea was—so rough as to make the passage of the bar impossible, and any change for the worse in the weather would probably drive his own crazy ships ashore and cut off all hope of escape.

The Admiral, whose health was now permanently broken, and who only had respite from his sufferings in fine weather and when he was relieved from a burden of anxieties such as had been continually pressing on him now for three months, fell into his old state of sleeplessness, feverishness, and consequent depression; and it, these circumstances it is not wonderful that the firm ground of fact began to give a little beneath him and that his feet began to sink again into the mire or quag of stupor. Of these further flounderings in the quag he himself wrote an account to the King and Queen, so we may as well have it in his own words.

"I mounted to the top of the ship crying out with a weak voice, weeping bitterly, to the commanders of your Majesties' army, and calling again to the four winds to help; but they did not answer me. Tired out, I fell asleep and sighing I heard a voice very full of pity which spoke these words: O fool! and slow to believe and to serve Him, thy God and the God of all. What did He more for Moses? and for David His servant? Since thou wast born He had always so great care for thee. When He saw thee in an age with which He was content He made thy name sound marvellously through the world. The Indies, which are so rich apart of the world, He has given to thee as thine. Thou hast distributed them wherever it has pleased thee; He gave thee power so to do. Of the bonds of the ocean which were locked with so strong chains He gave thee the keys, and thou wast obeyed in all the land, and among the Christians thou hast acquired a good and honourable reputation. What did He more for the people of Israel when He brought them out of Egypt? or yet for David, whom from being a shepherd He made King of Judea? Turn to Him and recognise thine error, for His mercy is infinite. Thine old age will be no hindrance to all great things. Many very great inheritances are in His power. Abraham was more than one hundred years old when he begat Isaac and also Sarah was not young. Thou art calling for uncertain aid. Answer me, who has afflicted thee so much and so many times—God or the world? The privileges and promises which God makes He never breaks to any one; nor does He say after having received the service that His intention was not so and it is to be understood in another manner: nor imposes martyrdom to give proof of His power. He abides by the letter of His word. All that He promises He abundantly accomplishes. This is His way. I have told thee what the Creator hath done for thee and does for all. Now He shows me the reward and payment of thy suffering and which thou hast passed in the service of others. And thus half dead, I heard everything; but I could never find an answer to make to words so certain, and only I wept for my errors. He, who ever he might be, finished speaking, saying: Trust and fear not, for thy tribulations are written in marble and not without reason."

Mere darkness of stupor; not much to be deciphered from it, nor any profitable comment to be made on it, except that it was our poor Christopher's way of crying out his great suffering and misery. We must not notice it, much as we should like to hold out a hand of sympathy and comfort to him; must not pay much attention to this dark eloquent nonsense—merely words, in which the Admiral never does himself justice. Acts are his true conversation; and when he speaks in that language all men must listen.

CHAPTER IV

HEROIC ADVENTURES BY LAND AND SEA

No man ever had a better excuse for his superstitions than the Admiral; no sooner had he got done with his Vision than the wind dropped, the sun came out, the sea fell, and communication with the land was restored. While he had been sick and dreaming one of his crew, Diego Mendez, had been busy with practical efforts in preparation for this day of fine weather; he had made a great raft out of Indian canoes lashed together, with mighty sacks of sail cloth into which the provisions might be bundled; and as soon as the sea had become calm enough he took this raft in over the bar to the settlement ashore, and began the business of embarking the whole of the stores and ammunition of Bartholomew's garrison. By this practical method the whole establishment was transferred from the shore to the ships in the space of two days, and nothing was left but the caravel, which it was found impossible to float again. It was heavy work towing the raft constantly backwards and forwards from the ships to the shore, but Diego Mendez had the satisfaction of being the last man to embark from the deserted settlement, and to see that not an ounce of stores or ammunition had been lost.

Columbus, always quick to reward the services of a good man, kissed Diego Mendez publicly—on both cheeks, and (what doubtless pleased him much better) gave him command of the caravel of which poor Tristan had been the captain.

With a favourable wind they sailed from this accursed shore at the end of April 1503. It is strange, as Winsor points out, that in the name of this coast should be preserved the only territorial remembrance of Columbus, and that his descendant the Duke of Veragua should in his title commemorate one of the most unfortunate of the Admiral's adventures. And if any one should desire a proof of the utterly misleading nature of most of Columbus's writings about himself, let him know that a few months later he solemnly wrote to the Sovereigns concerning this very place that "there is not in the world a country whose inhabitants are more timid; and the whole place is capable of being easily put into a state of defence. Your people that may come here, if they should wish to become masters of the products of other lands, will have to take them by force or retire empty-handed. In this country they will simply have to trust their persons in the hands of the savages." The facts being that the inhabitants were extremely fierce and warlike and irreconcilably hostile; that the river was a trap out of which in the dry season there was no escape, and the harbour outside a mere shelterless lee shore; that it would require an army and an armada to hold the place against the natives, and that any one who trusted himself in their hands would share the fate of the unhappy Diego Tristan. One may choose between believing that the Admiral's memory had entirely failed him (although he had not been backward in making a minute record, of all his sufferings) or that he was craftily attempting to deceive the Sovereigns. My own belief is that he was neither trying to deceive anybody nor that he had forgotten anything, but that he was simply incapable of uttering the bare truth when he had a pen in his hand.

From their position on the coast of Veragua Espanola bore almost due north; but Columbus was too good a seaman to attempt to make the island by sailing straight for it. He knew that the steady west-going current would set him far down on his course, and he therefore decided to work up the coast a long way to the eastward before standing across for Espanola. The crew grumbled very much at this proceeding, which they did not understand; in fact they argued from it that the Admiral was making straight for Spain, and this, in the crazy condition of the vessels, naturally alarmed them. But in his old high-handed, secret way the Admiral told them nothing; he even took away from the other captains all the charts that they had made of this coast, so that no one but himself would be able to find the way back to it; and he took a kind of pleasure in the complete mystification thus produced on his fellow-voyagers. "None of them could explain whither I went nor whence I came; they did not know the way to return thither," he writes, somewhat childishly.

But he was not back in Espanola yet, and his means for getting there were crumbling away beneath his feet. One of the three remaining caravels was entirely riddled by seaworms and had to be abandoned at the harbour called Puerto Bello; and the company was crowded on to two ships. The men now became more than ever discontented at the easterly course, and on May 1st, when he had come as far east as the Gulf of Darien, Columbus felt obliged to bear away to the north, although as it turned out he had not nearly made enough easting. He stood on this course, for nine days, the west-going current setting him down all the time; and the first land that he made, on May 10th, was the group of islands off the western end of Cuba which he had called the Queen's Gardens.

He anchored for six days here, as the crews were completely exhausted; the ships' stores were reduced to biscuits, oil, and vinegar; the vessels leaked like sieves, and the pumps had to be kept going continually. And no sooner had they anchored than a hurricane came on, and brought up a sea so heavy that the Admiral was convinced that his ships could not live within it. We have got so accustomed to reading of storms and tempests that it seems useless to try and drive home the horror and terror of them; but here were these two rotten ships alone at the end of the world, far beyond the help of man, the great seas roaring up under them in the black night, parting their worn cables, snatching away their anchors from them, and finally driving them one upon the other to grind and strain and prey upon each other, as though the external conspiracy of the elements against them both were not sufficient! One writes or reads the words, but what does it mean to us? and can we by any conceivable effort of imagination realise what it meant to this group of human beings who lived through that night so many hundred years ago—men like ourselves with hearts to sink and faint, capable of fear and hunger, capable of misery, pain, and endurance? Bruised and battered, wet by the terrifying surges, and entirely uncomforted by food or drink, they did somehow endure these miseries; and were to endure worse too before they were done with it.

Their six days' sojourn amid the Queen's Gardens, then, was not a great success; and as soon as they were able they set sail again, standing eastward when the wind permitted them. But wind and current were against them and all through the month of May and the early part of June they struggled along the south coast of Cuba, their ships as full of holes as a honeycomb, pumps going incessantly, and in addition the worn-out seamen doing heroic labour at baling with buckets and kettles. Lee helm! Down go the buckets and kettles and out run the wretched scarecrows of seamen to the weary business of tacking ship, letting go, brailing up, hauling in, and making fast for the thousandth time; and then back to the pumps and kettles again. No human being could endure this for an indefinite time; and though their diet of worms represented by the rotten biscuit was varied with cassava bread supplied by friendly natives, the Admiral could not make his way eastward further than Cape Cruz. Round that cape his leaking, strained vessels could not be made to look against the wind and the tide. Could hardly indeed be made to float or swim upon the water at all; and the Admiral had now to consider, not whether he could sail on a particular point of the compass, but whether he could by any means avoid another course which the fates now proposed to him—namely, a perpendicular course to the bottom of the sea. It was a race between the water and the ships, and the only thing the Admiral could think of was to turn southward across to Jamaica, which he did on June 23rd, putting into Puerto Bueno, now called Dry Harbour. But there was no food there, and as his ships were settling deeper and deeper in the water he had to make sail again and drive eastwards as far as Puerto Santa Gloria, now called Don Christopher's Cove. He was just in time. The ships were run ashore side by side on a sandy beach, the pumps were abandoned, and in one tide the ships were full of water. The remaining anchor cables were used to lash the two ships together so that they would not move; although there was little fear of that, seeing the weight of water that was in

43

them. Everything that could be saved was brought up on deck, and a kind of cabin or platform which could be fortified was rigged on the highest part of the ships. And so no doubt for some days, although their food was almost finished, the wretched and exhausted voyagers could stretch their cramped limbs, and rest in the warm sun, and listen, from their safe haven on the firm sands, to the hated voice of the sea.

Thanks to careful regulations made by the Admiral, governing the intercourse between the Spaniards and the natives ashore, friendly relations were soon established, and the crews were supplied with cassava bread and fruit in abundance. Two officials superintended every purchase of provisions to avoid the possibility of any dispute, for in the event of even a momentary hostility the thatched-roof structures on the ships could easily have been set on fire, and the position of the Spaniards, without shelter amid a hostile population, would have been a desperate one. This disaster, however, was avoided; but the Admiral soon began to be anxious about the supply of provisions from the immediate neighbourhood, which after the first few days began to be irregular. There were a large number of Spaniards to be fed, the natives never kept any great store of provisions for themselves, and the Spaniards were entirely at their mercy for, provisions from day to day. Diego Mendez, always ready for active and practical service, now offered to take three men and make a journey through the island to arrange for the purchase of provisions from different villages, so that the men on the ships would not be dependent upon any one source. This offer was gratefully accepted; and Mendez, with his lieutenants well supplied with toys and trinkets, started eastward along the north coast of Jamaica. He made no mistakes; he was quick and clever at ingratiating himself with the caciques, and he succeeded in arranging with three separate potentates to send regular supplies of provisions to the men on the ships. At each place where he made this arrangement he detached one of his assistants and sent him back with the first load of provisions, so that the regular line of carriage might be the more quickly established; and when they had all gone he borrowed a couple of natives and pushed on by himself until he reached the eastern end of the island. He made friends here with a powerful cacique named Amerro, from whom he bought a large canoe, and paid for it with some of the clothing off his back. With the canoe were furnished six Indians to row it, and Mendez made a triumphant journey back by sea, touching at the places where his depots had been established and seeing that his commissariat arrangements were working properly. He was warmly received on his return to the ships, and the result of his efforts was soon visible in the daily supplies of food that now regularly arrived.

Thus was one difficulty overcome; but it was not likely that either Columbus himself or any of his people would be content to remain for ever on the beach of Jamaica. It was necessary to establish communication with Espanola, and thence with Spain; but how to do it in the absence of ships or even boats? Columbus, pondering much upon this matter, one day calls Diego Mendez aside; walks him off, most likely, under the great rustling trees beyond the beach, and there tells him his difficulty. "My son," says he, "you and I understand the difficulties and dangers of our position here better than any one else. We are few; the Indians are many; we know how fickle and easily irritated they are, and how a fire-brand thrown into our thatched cabins would set the whole thing ablaze. It is quite true that you have very cleverly established a provision supply, but it is dependent entirely upon the good nature of the natives and it might cease to-morrow. Here is my plan: you have a good canoe; why should some one not go over to Espanola in it and send back a ship for us?"

Diego Mendez, knowing very well what is meant, looks down upon the ground. His spoken opinion is that such a journey is not merely difficult but impossible journey in a frail native canoe across one hundred and fifty miles of open and rough sea; although his private opinion is other than that. No, he cannot imagine such a thing being done; cannot think who would be able to do it.

Long silence from the Admiral; eloquent silence, accompanied by looks no less eloquent.

"Admiral," says Mendez again, "you know very well that I have risked my life for you and the people before and would do it again. But there are others who have at least as good a right to this great honour and peril as I have; let me beg of you, therefore, to summon all the company together, make this proposal to them, and see if any one will undertake it. If not, I will once more risk my life."

The proposal being duly made to the assembled crews, every one, as cunning Mendez had thought, declares it impossible; every one hangs back. Upon which Diego Mendez with a fine gesture comes forward and volunteers; makes his little dramatic effect and has his little ovation. Thoroughly Spanish this, significant of that mixture of vanity and bravery, of swagger and fearlessness, which is characteristic of the best in Spain. It was a desperately brave thing to venture upon, this voyage from Jamaica to Espanola in a native canoe and across a sea visited by dreadful hurricanes; and the volunteer was entitled to his little piece of heroic drama.

While Mendez was making his preparations, putting a false keel on the canoe and fixing weather boards along its gunwales to prevent its shipping seas, fitting a mast and sail and giving it a coat of tar, the Admiral retired into his cabin and busied himself with his pen. He wrote one letter to Ovando briefly describing his circumstances and requesting that a ship should be sent for his relief; and another to the Sovereigns, in which a long rambling account was given of the events of the voyage, and much other matter besides, dismally eloquent of his floundering in the quag. Much in it—about Solomon and Josephus, of the Abbot Joachim, of Saint Jerome and the Great Khan; more about the Holy Sepulchre and the intentions of the Almighty in that matter; with some serious practical concern for the rich land of Veragua which he had discovered, lest it should share the fate of his other discoveries and be eaten up by idle adventurers. "Veragua," he says, "is not a little son which may be given to a stepmother to nurse. Of Espanola and Paria and all the other lands I never think without the tears falling from my eyes; I believe that the example of these ought to serve for the others." And then this passage:

"The good and sound purpose which I always had to serve your Majesties, and the dishonour and unmerited ingratitude, will not suffer the soul to be silent although I wished it, therefore I ask pardon of your Majesties. I have been so lost and undone; until now I have wept for others that your Majesties might have compassion on them; and now may the heavens weep for me and the earth weep for me in temporal affairs; I have not a farthing to make as an offering in spiritual affairs. I have remained here on the Indian islands in the manner I have before said in great pain and infirmity, expecting every day death, surrounded by innumerable savages full of cruelty and by our enemies, and so far from the sacraments of the Holy Mother Church that I believe the soul will be forgotten when it leaves the body. Let them weep for me who have charity, truth and justice. I did not undertake this voyage of navigation to gain honour or material things, that is certain, because the hope already was entirely lost; but I did come to serve your Majesties with honest intention and with good charitable zeal, and I do not lie."

Poor old heart, older than its years, thus wailing out its sorrows to ears none too sympathetic; sad old voice, uplifted from the bright shores of that lonely island in the midst of strange seas! It will not come clear to the head alone; the echoes of this cry must reverberate in the heart if they are to reach and animate the understanding.

At this time also the Admiral wrote to his friend Gaspar Gorricio. For the benefit of those who may be interested I give the letter in English.

REVEREND AND VERY DEVOUT FATHER:

"If my voyage should be as conducive to my personal health and the repose of my house as it seems likely to be conducive to the aggrandisement of the royal Crown of the King and Queen, my Lords, I might hope to live more than a hundred years. I have not time to write more at length. I hope that the bearer of this letter may be a person of my house who will tell you verbally more than can be told in a thousand papers, and also Don Diego will supply information. I beg as a favour of the Father Prior and all the members of your religious house, that they remember me in all their prayers.

"Done on the island of Jamaica, July 7, 1503.
"I am at the command of your Reverence.

.S.
.S.A.S. XMY
Xpo FERENS."

Diego Mendez found some one among the Spaniards to accompany him, but his name is not recorded. The six Indians were taken to row the canoe. They had to make their way at first against the strong currents along the northern coast of Jamaica, so as to reach its eastern extremity before striking across to Espanola. At one point they met a flotilla of Indian canoes, which chased them and captured them, but they escaped. When they arrived at the end of the easterly point of Jamaica, now known as Morant Point, they had to wait two or three days for calm weather and a favourable wind to waft them across to Espanola, and while thus waiting they were suddenly surrounded and captured by a tribe of hostile natives, who carried them off some nine or ten miles into the island, and signified their intention of killing them.

But they began to quarrel among themselves as to how they should divide the spoils which they had captured with the canoe, and decided that the only way of settling the dispute was by some elaborate trial of hazard which they used. While they were busy with their trial Diego Mendez managed to escape, got back to the canoe, and worked his way back in it alone to the harbour where the Spaniards were encamped. The other Spaniard who was with him probably perished, for there is no record of what became of him—an obscure life lost in a brave enterprise.

One would have thought that Mendez now had enough of canoe voyages, but he had no sooner got back than he offered to set out again, only stipulating that an armed force should march along the coast by land to secure his safety until he could stand across to Espanola. Bartholomew Columbus immediately put himself at the head of a large and well-armed party for this purpose, and Bartolomeo Fieschi, the Genoese captain of one of the lost caravels, volunteered to accompany Mendez in a second canoe. Each canoe was now manned by six Spanish volunteers and ten Indians to row; Fieschi, as soon as they had reached the coast of Espanola, was to bring the good news to the Admiral; while Mendez must go on to San Domingo, procure a ship, and himself proceed to Spain with the Admiral's letters. The canoes were provisioned with water, cassava bread, and fish; and they departed on this enterprise some time in August 1503.

Their passage along the coast was protected by Bartholomew Columbus, who marched along with them on the shore. They waited a few days at the end of the island for favourable weather, and finally said farewell to the good Adelantado, who we may be sure stood watching them until they were well out of sight.

There was not a cloud in the sky when the canoes stood out to sea; the water was calm, and reflected the blistering heat of the sun. It was not a pleasant situation for people in an open boat; and Mendez and Fieschi were kept busy, as Irving says, "animating the Indians who navigated their canoes, and who frequently paused at their labour." The poor Indians, evidently much in need of such animation, would often jump into the water to escape the intolerable heat, and after a short immersion there would return to their task. Things were better when the sun went down, and the cool night came on; half the Indians then slept and half rowed, while half of the Spaniards also slept and the other half, I suppose, "animated." Irving also says that the animating half "kept guard with their weapons in hand, ready to defend themselves in the case of any perfidy on the part of their savage companions"; such perfidy being far enough from the thoughts of the savage companions, we may imagine, whose energies were entirely occupied with the oars.

The next day was the same: savage companions rowing, Spaniards animating; Spaniards and savage companions alike drinking water copiously without regard for the smallness of their store. The second night was very hot, and the savage companions finished the water, with the result that on the third day the thirst became a torment, and at mid-day the poor companions struck work. Artful Mendez, however, had concealed two small kegs of water in his canoe, the contents of which he now administered in small doses, so that the poor Indians were enabled to take to their oars again, though with vigour much abated. Presumably the Spaniards had put up their weapons by this time, for the only perfidy shown on the part of the savage companions was that one of them died in the following night and had to be thrown overboard, while others lay panting on the bottom of the canoes; and the Spaniards had to take their turn at the oars, although they were if anything in a worse case than the Indians.

Late in the night, however, the moon rose, and Mendez had the joy of seeing its lower disc cut by a jagged line which proved to be the little islet or rock of Navassa, which lies off the westerly end of Espanola. New hope now animated the sufferers, and they pushed on until they were able to land on this rock, which proved to be without any vegetation whatsoever, but on the surface of which there were found some precious pools of rain-water. Mendez was able to restrain the frantic appetites of his fellow-countrymen, but the savage companions were less wise, and drank their fill; so that some of them died in torment on the spot, and others became seriously ill. The Spaniards were able to make a fire of driftwood, and boil some shell-fish, which they found on shore, and they wisely spent the heat of the day crouching in the shade of the rocks, and put off their departure until the evening. It was then a comparatively easy journey for them to cross the dozen miles that separated them from Espanola, and they landed the next day in a pleasant harbour near Cape Tiburon. Fieschi, true to his promise, was then ready to start back for Jamaica with news of the safe accomplishment of the voyage; but the remnant of the crews, Spaniards and savage companions alike, had had enough of it, and no threats or persuasions would induce them to embark again. Mendez, therefore, left his friends to enjoy some little repose before continuing their journey to San Domingo, and, taking six natives of Espanola to row his canoe; set off along the coast towards the capital. He had not gone half-way when he learned that Ovando was not there, but was in Xaragua, so he left his canoe and struck northward through the forest until he arrived at the Governor's camp.

Ovando welcomed Mendez cordially, praised him for his plucky voyage, and expressed the greatest concern at the plight of the Admiral; but he was very busy at the moment, and was on the point of transacting a piece of business that furnished a dismal proof of the deterioration which had taken place in him. Anacaona—the lady with the daughter whom we remember—was now ruling over the province of Xaragua, her brother having died; and as perhaps her native subjects had been giving a little trouble to the Governor, he had come to exert his authority. The narrow official mind, brought into contact with native life, never develops in the direction of humanity; and Ovando had now for some time made the great discovery that it was less trouble to kill people than to try to rule over them wisely. There had evidently always been a streak of Spanish cruelty in him, which had been much developed by his residence in Espanola; and to cruelty and narrow officialdom he now added treachery of a very monstrous and horrible kind.

He announced his intention of paying a state visit to Anacaona, who thereupon summoned all her tributary chiefs to a kind of levee held in his honour. In the midst of the levee, at a given signal, Ovando's soldiers rushed in, seized the caciques, fastened them to the wooden pillars of the house, and set the whole thing on fire; the caciques being thus miserably roasted alive. While this was going on the atrocious work was completed by the soldiers massacring every native they could see — children, women, and old men included—and Anacaona herself was taken and hanged.

All these things Diego Mendez had to witness; and when they were over, Ovando still had excuses for not hurrying to the relief of the Admiral. He had embarked on a campaign of extermination against the natives, and he followed up his atrocities at Xaragua by an expedition to the eastern end of Espanola, where very much the same kind of business was transacted. Weeks and months passed in this bloody cruelty, and there was always an excuse for putting off Mendez. Now it was because of the operations which he dignified by the name of wars, and now because he had no ship suitable for sending to Jamaica; but the truth was that Ovando, the springs of whose humanity had been entirely dried up during his disastrous reign in Espanola, did not want Columbus to see with his own eyes the terrible state of the island, and was callous enough to leave him either to perish or to find his own way back to the world. It was only when news came that a fleet of caravels was expected from Spain that Ovando could no longer prevent Mendez from going to San Domingo and, purchasing one of them.

Ovando had indeed lost all but the outer semblance of a man; the soul or animating part of him had entirely gone to corruption. He had no interest in rescuing the Admiral; he had, on the contrary, great interest in leaving him unrescued; but curiosity as to his fate, and fear as to his actions in case he should return to Espanola, induced the Governor to make some effort towards spying cut his condition. He had a number of trained rascals under his command—among them Diego de Escobar, one of Roldan's bright brigade; and Ovando had no sooner seen Mendez depart on his journey to San Domingo than he sent this Escobar to embark in a small caravel on a visit to Jamaica in order to see if the Admiral was still alive. The caravel had to be small, so that there could be no chance of bringing off the 130 men who had been left to perish there; and various astute instructions were given to Escobar in order to prevent his arrival being of any comfort or assistance to the shipwrecked ones. And so Escobar sailed; and so, in the month of March 1504, eight months after the vanishing of Mendez below the eastern horizon, the miserable company encamped on the two decaying ships on the sands at Puerto Santa Gloria descried with joyful excitement the sails of a Spanish caravel standing in to the shore.

CHAPTER V

THE ECLIPSE OF THE MOON

We must now return to the little settlement on the coast of Jamaica —those two wornout caravels, lashed together with ropes and bridged by an erection of wood and thatch, in which the forlorn little company was established. In all communities of men so situated there are alternate periods of action and reaction, and after the excitement incidental to the departure of Mendez, and the return of Bartholomew with the news that he had got safely away, there followed a time of reaction, in which the Spaniards looked dismally out across the empty sea and wondered when, if ever, their salvation would come. Columbus himself was now a confirmed invalid, and could hardly ever leave his bed under the thatch; and in his own condition of pain and depression his influence on the rest of the crew must inevitably have been less inspiriting than it had formerly been. The men themselves, moreover, began to grow sickly, chiefly on account of the soft vegetable food, to which they were not accustomed, and partly because of their cramped quarters and the moist, unhealthy climate, which was the very opposite of what they needed after their long period of suffering and hardship at sea.

As the days and weeks passed, with no occupation save the daily business of collecting food that gradually became more and more nauseous to them, and of straining their eyes across the empty blue of the sea in an anxious search for the returning canoes of Fieschi, the spirits of the castaways sank lower and lower. Inevitably their discontent became articulate and broke out into murmurings. The usual remedy for this state of affairs is to keep the men employed at some hard work; but there was no work for them to do, and the spirit of dissatisfaction had ample opportunity to spread. As usual it soon took the form of hostility to the Admiral. They seem to have borne him no love or gratitude for his masterly guiding of them through so many dangers; and now when he lay ill and in suffering his treacherous followers must needs fasten upon him the responsibility for their condition. After a month or two had passed, and it became certain that Fieschi was not coming back, the castaways could only suppose that he and Mendez had either been captured by natives or had perished at sea, and that their fellow-countrymen must still be without news of the Admiral's predicament. They began to say also that the Admiral was banished from Spain; that there was no desire or intention on the part of the Sovereigns to send an expedition to his relief; even if they had known of his condition; and that in any case they must long ago have given him up for lost.

When the pot boils the scum rises to the surface, and the first result of these disloyal murmurings and agitations was to bring into prominence the two brothers, Francisco and Diego de Porras, who, it will be remembered, owed their presence with the expedition entirely to the Admiral's good nature in complying with the request of their brother-in-law Morales, who had apparently wished to find some distant occupation for them. They had been given honourable posts as officers, in which they had not proved competent; but the Admiral had always treated them with kindness and courtesy, regarding them more as guests than as servants. Who or what these Porras brothers were, where they came from, who were their father and mother, or what was their training, I do not know; it is enough for us to know that the result of it all had been the production of a couple of very mean scoundrels, who now found an opportunity to exercise their scoundrelism.

When they discovered the nature of the murmuring and discontent among the crew they immediately set them to work it up into open mutiny. They represented that, as Mendez had undoubtedly perished, there was no hope of relief from Espanola; that the Admiral did not even expect such relief, knowing that the island was forbidden ground to him. They insinuated that he was as well content to remain in Jamaica as anywhere else, since he had to undergo a period of banishment until his friends at Court could procure his forgiveness. They were all, said the Porras brothers, being made tools for the Admiral's convenience; as he did not wish to leave Jamaica himself, he was keeping them all there, to perish as likely as not, and in the meantime to form a bodyguard, and establish a service for himself. The Porras brothers suggested that, under these circumstances, it would be as well to take a fleet of native canoes from the Indians and make their own way to Espanola; the Admiral would never undertake the voyage himself, being too helpless from the gout; but it would be absurd if the whole company were to be allowed to perish because of the infirmities of one man. They reminded the murmurers that they would not be the first people who had rebelled with success against the despotic rule of Columbus, and that the conduct of the Sovereigns on a former occasion afforded them some promise that those who rebelled again would receive something quite different from punishment.

Christmas passed, the old year went out in this strange, unhomelike place, and the new year came in. The Admiral, as we have seen, was now almost entirely crippled and confined to his bed; and he was lying alone in his cabin on the second day of the year when Francisco de Porras abruptly entered. Something very odd and flurried about Porras; he jerks and stammers, and suddenly breaks out into a flood of agitated speech, in which the Admiral distinguishes a stream of bitter reproach and impertinence. The thing forms itself into nothing more or less than a hurried, gabbling complaint; the people are dissatisfied at being kept here week after week with no hope of relief; they accuse the Admiral of neglecting their interests; and so on. Columbus, raising himself in his bed, tries to pacify Porras; gives him reasons why it is impossible for them to depart in canoes; makes every endeavour, in short, to bring this miserable fellow back to his duties. He is watching Porras's eye all the time; sees that he is too excited to be pacified by reason, and suspects that he has considerable support behind him; and suggests that the crew had better all be assembled and a consultation held as to the best course to pursue.

It is no good to reason with mutineers; and the Admiral has no sooner made this suggestion than he sees that it was a mistake. Porras scoffs at it; action, not consultation, is what he demands; in short he presents an ultimatum to the Admiral— either to embark with the whole company at once, or stay behind in Jamaica at his own pleasure. And then, turning his back on Columbus and raising his voice, he calls out, "I am for Castile; those who choose may follow me!"

The shout was a signal, and immediately from every part of the vessel resounded the voices of the Spaniards, crying out that they would follow Porras. In the midst of the confusion Columbus hobbled out of his bed and staggered on to the deck; Bartholomew seized his weapons and prepared for action; but the whole of the crew was not mutinous, and there was a large enough loyal remnant to make it unwise for the chicken-hearted mutineers to do more for the moment than shout: Some of them, it is true, were heard threatening the life of the Admiral, but he was hurried back to his bed by a few of the faithful ones, and others of them rushed up to the fierce Bartholomew, and with great difficulty persuaded him to drop his lance and retire to Christopher's cabin with him while they dealt with the offenders. They begged Columbus to let the scoundrels go if they wished to, as the condition of those who remained would be improved rather than hurt by their absence, and they would be a good riddance. They then went back to the deck and told Porras and his followers that the sooner they went the better, and that nobody would interfere with their going as long as they offered no one any violence.

The Admiral had some time before purchased some good canoes from the natives, and the mutineers seized ten of these and loaded them with native provisions. Every effort was made to add to the number of the disloyal ones; and when they saw their friends making ready to depart several of these did actually join. There were forty-eight who finally embarked with the brothers Porras; and there would have been more, but that so many of them were sick and unable to face the exposure of the voyage. As it was, those who remained witnessed with no very cheerful emotions the departure of their companions, and even in some cases fell to tears and lamentations. The poor old Admiral struggled out of his bed again, went round among the sick and the loyal, cheering them and comforting them, and promising to use every effort of the power left to him to secure an adequate reward for their loyalty when he should return to Spain.

We need only follow the career of Porras and his deserters for the present far enough to see them safely off the premises and out of the way of the Admiral and our narrative. They coasted along the shore of Jamaica to the eastward as Mendez had done, landing whenever they had a mind to, and robbing and outraging the natives; and they took a particularly mean and dirty revenge on the Admiral by committing all their robbings and outragings as though under his authority, assuring the offended Indians that what they did they did by his command and that what they took he would pay for; so that as they went along they sowed seeds of grievance and hostility against the Admiral. They told the natives, moreover, that Columbus was an enemy of all Indians, and that they would be very well advised to kill him and get him out of the way.

They had not managed very well with the navigation of the canoes; and while they were waiting for fine weather at the eastern end of the island they collected a number of natives to act as oarsmen. When they thought the weather suitable they put to sea in the direction of Espanola. They were only about fifteen miles from the shore, however, when the wind began to head them and to send up something of a sea; not rough, but enough to make the crank and overloaded canoes roll heavily, for they had not been prepared, as those of Mendez were, with false keels and weather-boards. The Spaniards got frightened and turned back to Jamaica; but the sea became rougher, the canoes rolled more and more, they often shipped a quantity of water, and the situation began to look serious. All their belongings except arms and provisions were thrown overboard; but still, as the wind rose and the sea with it, it became obvious that unless the canoes were further lightened they would not reach the shore in safety. Under these circumstances the Spaniards forced the natives to leap into the water, where they swam about like rats as well as they could, and then came back to the canoes in order to hold on and rest themselves. When they did this the Spaniards slashed at them with their swords or cut off their hands, so that one by one they fell back and, still swimming about feebly as well as they could with their bleeding hands or stumps of arms, the miserable wretches perished and sank at last.

By this dreadful expedient the Spaniards managed to reach Jamaica again, and when they landed they immediately fell to quarrelling as to what they should do next. Some were for trying to make the island of Cuba, the wind being favourable for that direction; others were for returning and making their submission to the Admiral; others for going back and seizing the remainder of his arms and stores; others for staying where they were for the present, and making another attempt to reach Espanola when the weather should be more favourable. This last plan, being the counsel of present inaction, was adopted by the majority of the rabble; so they settled themselves at a neighbouring Indian village, behaving in: the manner with which we are familiar. A little later, when the weather was calm, they made another attempt at the voyage, but were driven back in the same way; and being by this time sick of canoe voyages, they abandoned the attempt, and began to wander back westward through the island, maltreating the natives as before, and sowing seeds of bitter rancour and hostility against the Admiral; in whose neighbourhood we shall unfortunately hear of them again.

In the meantime their departure had somewhat relieved the condition of affairs on board the hulks. There were more provisions and there was more peace; the Admiral, rising above his own infirmities to the necessities of the occasion, moved unweariedly among the sick, cheering them and nursing them back into health and good humour, so that gradually the condition of the little colony was brought into better order and health than it had enjoyed since its establishment.

But now unfortunately the evil harvest sown by the Porras gang in their journey to the east of the island began to ripen. The supplies of provisions, which had hitherto been regularly brought by the natives, began to appear with less punctuality, and to fall off both in quantity and quality. The trinkets with which they were purchased had now been distributed in such quantities that they began to lose their novelty and value; sometimes the natives demanded a much higher price for the provisions they brought, and (having by this time acquired the art of bargaining) would take their stores away again if they did not get the price they asked.

But even of this device they soon grew weary; from being irregular, the supplies of provisions from some quarters ceased altogether, and the possibilities of famine began to stare the unhappy castaways in the face. It must be remembered that they were in a very weak physical condition, and that among the so-called loyal remnant there were very few who were not invalids; and they were unable to get out into the island and forage for themselves. If the able-bodied handful were to sally forth in search of provisions, the hulks would be left defenceless and at the mercy of the natives, of whose growing hostility the Admiral had by this time discovered abundant evidence. Thus little by little the food supply diminished until there was practically nothing left, and the miserable company of invalids were confronted with the alternative of either dying of starvation or desperately attempting a canoe voyage.

It was from this critical situation that the spirit and resource of Columbus once more furnished a way of escape, and in these circumstances that he invented and worked a device that has since become famous—the great Eclipse Trick. Among his small library in the cabin of the ship was the book containing the astronomical tables of Regiomontanus; and from his study of this work he was aware that an eclipse of the moon was due on a certain date near at hand. He sent his Indian interpreter to visit the neighbouring caciques, summoning them to a great conference to be held on the evening of the eclipse, as the Admiral had matters of great importance to reveal to them. They duly arrived on the evening appointed; not the caciques alone, but large numbers of the native population, well prepared for whatever might take place. Columbus then addressed them through his interpreter, informing him that he was under the protection of a God who dwelt in the skies and who rewarded all who assisted him and punished all his enemies. He made an effective use of the adventures of Mendez and Porras, pointing out that Mendez, who took his voyage by the Admiral's orders, had got away in safety, but that Porras and his followers, who had departed in disobedience and mutiny, had been prevented by the heavenly power from achieving their object. He told them that his God was angry with them for their hostility and for their neglect to supply him with provisions; and that in token of his anger he was going to send them a dreadful punishment, as a sign of which they would presently see the moon change colour and lose its light, and the earth become dark.

This address was spun out as long as possible; but even so it was followed by an interval in which, we may be sure, Columbus anxiously eyed the serene orb of night, and doubtless prayed that Regiomontanus might not have made a mistake in his calculations. Some of the Indians were alarmed, some of them contemptuous; but it was pretty clearly realised on both sides that matters between them had come to a head; and probably if Regiomontanus, who had worked out these tables of figures and calculations so many years ago in his German home, had done his work carelessly or made a mistake, Columbus and his followers would have been massacred on the spot. But Regiomontanus, God bless him! had made no mistake. Sure enough, and punctually to the appointed time, the dark shadow began to steal over the moon's disc; its light gradually faded, and a ghostly darkness crept over the face of the world. Columbus, having seen that all was right with the celestial machinery, had retired to his cabin; and presently he found himself besieged there in the dark night by crowds of natives frantically bringing what provisions they had and protesting their intention of continuing to bring them for the rest of their lives. If only the Admiral would ask his God to forgive them, there was no limit to the amount of provisions that he might have! The Admiral, piously thankful, and perhaps beginning to enjoy the situation a little, kept himself shut up in his cabin as though communing with the implacable deity, while the darkness deepened over the land and the shore resounded with the howling and sobbing of the terrified natives. He kept a look-out on the sky; and when he saw that the eclipse was about to pass away, he came out and informed the natives that God had decided to pardon them on condition of their remaining faithful in the matter of provisions, and that as a sign of His mercy He would restore the light. The beautiful miracle went on through its changing phases; and, watching in the darkness, the terrified natives saw the silver edge of the moon appearing again, the curtain that had obscured it gradually rolling away, and land and sea lying visible to them and once more steeped in the serene light which they worshipped. It is likely that Christopher slept more soundly that night than he had slept for many nights before.

The End